WHAT DO ECONOMISTS KNOW?

What Do Economists Know?

Six Lectures on
Economics in the Crisis of Democracy

by

BENJAMIN HIGGINS
M.Sc. (Lond.), Ph.D. (Minnesota)

*Professor of Economics, McGill University
and former Ritchie Professor of Research in Economics,
University of Melbourne*

MELBOURNE UNIVERSITY PRESS

First published 1951

Wholly set up and printed in Australia by
Melbourne University Press, Carlton, N.3, Victoria

London and New York: Cambridge University Press

Registered in Australia for transmission by post as a book

FOREWORD

TWENTY YEARS AGO, a Research Chair of Economics was founded in the University of Melbourne. For a decade it was occupied by one of Australia's most eminent economists, Professor L. F. Giblin, and then remained vacant until Professor Benjamin Higgins was appointed in 1948. To occupy so dusty a seat required some courage in a professional economist, but courage is one of Professor Higgins' qualities.

He assures us that he contributes nothing new in this book, but he serves the intelligent layman whom he addresses all the better for that. Most laymen talk Economics for much of their time; but they do so without knowing where Economics begins and ends or what questions it can and cannot answer, and hence without knowing when to regard the economist and when to disregard him. The result is much futile debate and confusion.

Perhaps the confusion will not be resolved, but at least Professor Higgins is entirely competent to show where it lies and how great it is. His experience in Europe and U.S.A., his wide knowledge of modern economics, his ability to see where economists agree and where their differences really lie, amply equip him to tackle his difficult task. Moreover, since no local Australian bias handicaps him, his readers may be sure that he is speaking to no brief but his own. If they are laymen they should guess, and if professionals they should know, that although his time in Australia was too short, Professor Higgins has made an eminent contribution to Australian Economics.

A. B. RITCHIE

ACKNOWLEDGMENTS

THE FOLLOWING authors and publishers are thanked for permission to quote from copyright material: F. H. Knight, *The Ethics of Competition* (George Allen & Unwin Ltd.); James Edward Meade, *Planning and the Price Mechanism* (George Allen & Unwin Ltd.); J. W. N. Sullivan, *The Bases of Modern Science* (Ernest Benn Ltd.); John S. Gambs, *Beyond Supply and Demand* (Columbia University Press); Henry C. Simons, *Personal Income Taxation* (University of Chicago Press); The Chamber of Commerce of the United States, *The American Competitive Enterprise System;* Murray Constantine, *Swastika Night* (Victor Gollancz Ltd.); Frank W. Knight and Thornton W. Merriam, *The Economic Order and Religion* (Harper and Brothers); J. A. Schumpeter, *Capitalism, Socialism and Democracy* (Harper and Brothers); Wilhelm Röpke, *Civitas Humana* (William Hodge & Co. Ltd.); John D. Black *Parity, Parity, Parity* (Harvard University Press); J. M. Clark, *Alternatives to Serfdom* (Alfred Knopf, Inc.); *The Essentials of Lenin* (Lawrence & Wishart Ltd.); Norman Kemp Smith (ed.), Kant's *Critique of Pure Reason* (Macmillan & Co. Ltd.); J. M. Keynes, *General Theory of Employment, Interest and Money* (Macmillan & Co. Ltd.); Lionel Robbins, *Essay on the Nature and Significance of Economic Science* (Macmillan & Co. Ltd.); Lawrence R. Klein, *The Keynesian Revolution* (The Macmillan Company); John R. Commons, *Institutional Economics* (The Macmillan Company); B. S. Keirstead, *Theory of Economic Change* (The Macmillan Co. of Canada Ltd.); W. D. MacMillan, *Dynamics of Rigid Bodies* (McGraw-Hill Book Co. Inc.); Susan Stebbing, *Philosophy and the Physicists* (Methuen & Co. Ltd.); National Bureau of Economic Research Inc., *Economic Research and the Keynesian Thinking of Our Times;* Max Planck, *Where is Science Going?* (W. W. Norton & Co. Inc.); Carl Trueblood Chase, *The Evolution of Modern Physics* (Van Nostrand Co. Inc.); Thorstein Veblen, *The Place of Science in Modern Civilization* (Viking Press Inc.); E. R. Walker, *Australia in the World Depression* (Staples Press Ltd.); Thomas B. Brown, *Foundations of Modern Physics* (John Wiley & Sons Inc.).

PREFACE

WHEN AN ECONOMIST writes a book — even a small one — it is always worth asking, "For whom is this book intended?" The essays published in this volume were originally delivered as a series of public lectures at the University of Melbourne, the first lecture constituting my Inaugural Address in that University. The lectures are reproduced here substantially as they were given; some illustrative material has been added, and a certain amount of reorganization has been undertaken, but otherwise they are unchanged. The book is therefore directed primarily at the same public as the lectures — the community of "intelligent laymen". To the author, it seems extremely important for articulate and influential members of the public to understand the nature, scope, and significance of expert knowledge in the field of economics, so that they will help economists to attain the position in democratic societies where their power to do good is maximized and their power to do harm minimized. This book is primarily an attempt to define that position.

The "intelligent layman", however, includes the beginning student. The standard textbook on "principles" too seldom deals with such questions as scope and method of economics, the relation among "schools" of economic thought, objectives of policy, the relation of economic science to politics, social conflicts, and wars. As a result, the beginning student frequently fails completely to see the relation between things he is being taught — such as the "law of diminishing returns" and the "law of increasing elasticity of substitution" — and the burning political-economic issues of the day, as he encounters them in the press, on the radio, in his home, in his fraternity or club or college. It is hoped that this book will help to bridge this gap, and that it will accordingly find a place as a supplementary textbook in elementary courses. It is intended to be useful also in courses on methodology, economic policy, and the history of economic thought.

Finally, while the author would certainly not claim to

vii

make a "contribution to knowledge" in this volume, he trusts that professional economists will not find it altogether boring. Recent literature indicates considerable fuzziness of thought among economists as to the extent of their knowledge, the ends of economic policy, and the proper role of economists in the formulation and administration of economic policy. Perhaps this little book will help to clarify some of these issues.

CONTENTS

WHAT DO ECONOMISTS KNOW?

THE CONQUEST OF FEAR must be counted among the major victories in the forward march of human progress. Fear of the supernatural, then fear of Nature herself, has been forced to retreat before the advance of knowledge. We consider it uncivilized to cringe in terror before capriciously vengeful gods, who demonstrate their wrath and power in thunder, lightning, earthquakes, fires, and eclipses. Yet we suffer today from fears more pervasive and more demoralizing than the silliest superstitions of the most primitive societies. Worse, the things that frighten us today are monsters of our own creation — inflation, depression, social strife, revolution, and war. What a sad commentary on the present state of society that we should live, like Frankenstein, in constant fear of monsters we have ourselves constructed! Can science do nothing to banish these fears, as it has banished others?

To the degree that current fears originate in pure selfishness, there is not much that science can do about them. The scientist can only hope that discovery and promulgation of the truth will produce an awareness of the self-destructive nature of relentlessly selfish action. But to the extent that these fears are based on ignorance, their abolition is a scientific task. Ignorance is the scientist's special adversary. The scientist is continuously engaged in fighting two kinds of ignorance; his own, and the layman's. If ignorance is at the root of present fears, whose ignorance is it, scientist's or layman's?

Inflation and depression are economic phenomena; social strife, revolutions, and wars, while not uniquely economic in their causation, usually have some economic basis. If fear of these monsters is to be exorcised by scientists, the task must fall largely to economists. It is therefore highly pertinent to present problems to ask, "What do economists know?" Do they know enough to prevent depression and inflation, to diminish the degree of social conflict, and reduce the danger of revolution and war?

I shall argue in this series of lectures that they do. I shall conclude from this argument that economists should be given a chance to perform this task, by being accorded powers with respect to economic welfare similar to the powers of medical doctors with regard to physical welfare. I shall argue further that no economic *system* can in itself guarantee a high level of welfare, and that any economic system requires expert advice on economic policy if it is to achieve commonly accepted objectives. Finally, I shall argue that the formulation of economic policy by experts, and retention of essential democratic freedoms, requires increased economic sophistication of the electorate, modernized machinery of democratic government, and a new social ethics. This introductory lecture will be concerned with the nature of knowledge in economics, and with substantiating the economist's claim to be an expert in his field.

The Scope of Economics

We must first make clear what it is that economists study. Economics is frequently defined as the study of human behaviour as a relationship between a multiplicity of ends and scarce means that have alternative uses.[1] The advantage of this definition is that it neatly isolates the range of problems that are peculiarly "economic". If means are not scarce, and everyone has all of everything he wants, there is no economic problem. Even if means are scarce, but each one has only one use, no economic problem arises, because every unit of every kind of resource would then have to be used in a particular way, and no decisions regarding *allocation* of resources would have to be made. A society with a single end has no *economic* problems either. If, for example, the sole objective is to consume as much beer as possible, the only problem is the engineering one — how can available resources be organized so as to maximize the production of beer? — plus, perhaps, certain physiological problems.

The peculiarly *economic* problem thus emerges as the problem of choice in the allocation of resources for the

---

[1] Lionel Robbins, *An Essay on the Nature and Significance of Economic Science*, London 1940. p. 16.

satisfaction of wants. Taken literally, however, this definition of economics would include certain kinds of choice about which economists as such know very little. Beautiful, intelligent, and sweet-tempered girls are undeniably scarce; they have alternative uses; but their allocation among various suitors is not a phenomenon that economists can explain, nor even one that economists have tried to explain.[2] To limit economics to the range of phenomena with which economists are really concerned, we must add to the above definition the qualifying phrase "insofar as it affects the production and distribution of goods and services". In this context, goods and services are any want-satisfying things that are "paid for" by someone, whether an individual, a firm, or a government.[3]

In general, "paid for" means exchanged for money. Some economists have enjoyed analysing the "economic behaviour" of Robinson Crusoe on his island, "paying for" satisfaction of wants with his own time and energy; but this exercise has been performed for illustrative purposes, not for its own sake. Theories of barter play a very small role in economics,

---

[2] Professor Frank Knight is unperturbed by the implications of Robbins' definition. He is quite prepared to regard economics as a science dealing with human choice of all kinds: "For the purpose of defining economics the correct procedure would appear to be to start from the ordinary meaning of the verb to economize, that is, to use resources wisely in the achievement of *given* ends. In so far as the ends are viewed as given, as data, then all activity is economic. The question of the effectiveness of the adaptation of means is the only question to be asked regarding conduct, and economics is the one and all-inclusive science of conduct. From this point of view the problem of life becomes simply the economic problem, how to employ the existing and available supplies of all sorts of resources, human and material, natural and artificial, in producing the maximum *amount* of *want-satisfaction*, including the provision of new resources for increased value production insofar as the present population finds itself actually desiring future progress" (F. H. Knight, *The Ethics of Competition*, London 1935, pp. 34-35). To my knowledge, however, Knight and Robbins constitute a minority of two in this respect.

[3] Professor Robbins may feel that this qualification restricts economics to the "materialism" that he decries (*op. cit.* Chapter II). Such is not the case, however; for the qualification does not exclude any good or service entering into exchange transactions. Bibles and beer, music and matzas, lemons and lectures, are equally economic goods and services, and behaviour concerned with their production and distribution is economic behaviour. But a man's choice of friends, spouse, religion, or chess technique is not economic behaviour, because these things are not ordinarily "paid for". In any case, Robbins' concept of "material" is surely too narrow. Is a symphony less "material" than a cigarette? Both reduce ultimately to physical laws.

and even in barter economies there is a tendency for one or
a few commodities to emerge as units of account and so to
act as money. Thus if a young man acquires a bride in the
slave market the transaction is "economic", while if he wooes
and wins her it is not.[4]

This definition raises questions regarding the border lines
between economics and other social sciences, especially politics, history, sociology, and psychology. These questions have
been discussed at length in the literature on scope and
method of economics, and they will arise again in later
lectures of this series. Consequently, we shall deal with them
here in summary fashion.

Political science is concerned with human behaviour as
an effort to maximize political power. It analyses the functioning of political systems, and indulges in philosophical
speculations about the ideal form of political organization.[5]
When political scientists themselves make recommendations
for policy, they are presumably concerned with making
political systems more efficient in giving people what they
want, or perhaps what the political philosopher thinks they
ought to have. All this has nothing to do with economics.
The economist as such takes political systems as given. He
endeavours to develop laws sufficiently general to be valid
in *all* political systems; if economics is to be a science, there
cannot be a "socialist economics", a "fascist economics", and
a "capitalist economics". At the same time, the economist
recognizes the need to take account of the effects on economic
behaviour of the form of political organization.

These days, people seek to increase their power of disposal
over goods and services not only as individuals but as members of trade unions, employers' associations, farmers' associations and political parties. In so far as it affects the
production and distribution of goods and services, the

---

4 For further discussion of these points, see L. M. Fraser, *Economic Thought
and Language,* London 1937, Chapter 2.
5 The UNESCO project on Methods in Political Science defined it to include
political theory, national and local government, political parties and public
opinion, economic functions of government, comparative institutions and
international law and relations.

behaviour of such groups is economic and must be studied by economists. But the administrative process, the means used by political parties to get power, and theories about the ideal form of political organization are no concern of economists as economists. In recent years, it is true, economists have become painfully aware of the difficulties of obtaining effective economic action in democratic societies, and have taken an increasing interest in problems of public administration. However, when an economist is dealing with, say, the administrative requirements of a public investment programme to maintain full employment, he is not acting as an economist, but as an amateur political scientist. He may be quite a competent amateur, and political science may gain from an infusion of the method of economics; but the fact remains that the economist *as such* has no expert knowledge regarding the efficiency of various kinds of political organization, and can express no expert opinions regarding their relative desirability.

History is clearly concerned with human behaviour in a much broader context than economics. There is no aspect of human behaviour which the historian may not legitimately cover. Economic history, on the other hand, is a part of economics. It is concerned with arranging facts about economic behaviour according to their sequence in time. It may turn up unexplained facts, from which new sets of generalizations may be deduced, or it may provide empirical tests of deduced relationships. As Professor Robbins has pointed out, statistics are just a special way of writing history, and economic statistics are a part of economic history. If the economic statistician or historian deduces generalizations from his facts, thus suggesting causal relationships, he ceases to be merely an economic historian, and becomes a general economist.[6]

Economists have often been subject to criticism from sociologists, for a presumed failure to take account of the

6 Economic history is also, of course, a part of history. Cf. B. Higgins, review of W. W. Rostow, *British Economy of the Nineteenth Century*, in *The Economic Record*, June 1949.

effects of social institutions, mass psychology, prejudices,
public opinion, and the like on economic behaviour.[7] This
sort of criticism is relatively new, because specialization
within the social sciences is itself a relatively new phenomena.
Adam Smith, frequently considered the "father of political
economy", lectured in natural theology, ethics, national and
international law, arms and "police", or political economy.
Nearly one hundred years later, Stanley Jevons' chair at
Manchester embraced logic and mental and moral philosophy, as well as political economy. The effort to develop
an economics independent of the social framework is also
new. The classical school studied economic behaviour within
the framework of eighteenth- and nineteenth-century
capitalism. They made odd references to the undeveloped
economies of the Americas, to primitive societies, and to
Utopias, but they made no effort to show how economic laws
valid for capitalist economies might have to be modified if
applied to other societies, because they did not consider other
societies very important.

The "marginal revolution" of the 1870's, however, combined with the rise of "scientific socialism", led economists
of the late nineteenth century to claim for their economic
laws generality for all kinds of society, from Crusoe to Communism. It is these claims that prompts the counter-attack.
However, the criticisms are for the most part ill-founded.
The fundamental economic problem of allocating resources
so as to maximize satisfaction is the same in any society, and
there are certain economic laws which apply to all forms
of social organization. Economists are well aware of the
effects of customs, mores, group conflicts, and various institutions on economic behaviour. However, they regard these
factors as data; they are concerned only with their effects
on economic behaviour, and do not consider it their duty to
study how these phenomena arise.

There has probably been more confusion about the
relationship of economics to psychology than about any other
relationship among social sciences. The confusion is natural

---

[7] See, for example, Adolph Lowe, *Economics and Sociology: A Plea for Co-
operation in the Social Sciences*, London 1935, pp. 20 and 21.

enough. Psychology purports to study human behaviour, while economics studies human behaviour in one of its aspects. Such being the case, must not the concepts of economic behaviour be derived from laws discovered by psychologists? This question need not occupy us long. Economics and psychology each have their proper field of investigation, and there is only a very small degree of overlapping. The subject matter of psychiatry, for example, is no concern of the economist. The distinction between abnormal and normal behaviour is admittedly one of degree; but it is safe to say that economics deals with non-pathological behaviour. Economics is no more concerned with the nature and causes of oedipus complexes and schizophrenia than it is with the nature and causes of tuberculosis and angina pectoris. If a man buys a brown shirt for the conscious reason that he thinks it will look well with a certain suit, while the real but unconscious reason is a frustrated boyhood fixation on his Scout Leader, the man's neurosis is of no importance to the theory of price determination. The only important consideration for economic analysis is that, for *some* reason, he "prefers" the shirt to any other use of the guinea that it costs him; that is, he exchanges his guinea for the shirt.[8]

Similarly, the experimental psychologist is interested in matters of no direct significance to economics. A thorough knowledge of the structure of synapses or the function of the semi-circular canal, or the dispersion of cutaneous sensory nerve-centres and reaction-times, is neither necessary nor useful in the development of economic theory. Some psychologists have emphasised the importance of purely impulsive or reflex action. Even such actions are not lawless, however. And can any psychologist honestly assert that when he buys a tie, he sees the tie in the window, impulsively

---

8 E. R. Walker puts the case very well: "What can the economist do? Unfortunately, if he goes to any standard work on psychology, he is not likely to find any information that will help him to claim scientific objectivity for his interpretation of concrete situations. If he seeks light from the Freudians, he will find plenty of information, however incredible. But to learn that money is a well-known psychological symbol, and that the tightness (or looseness) of the money market reflects the anal eroticism of bankers, does not really solve the economist's difficulties" (*Australia in the World Depression*, London, 1933, p. 204).

enters the store, which stimulates him to ask for the tie, that a reflex action sends his hand into his pocket and brings it out with ten shillings, another impulse makes him take the tie, and that all the time he has no consciousness of what he is doing? As long as there is some reflection about the choice which is being made, no matter what the influences nor how casual the choice may be, it is enough for economic theory.

The field of psychology which would have the most significance for economic theory, if it existed, would be a "pure psychology", providing "laws" about individual reactions to given situations. How useful it would be, for example, to know whether a fall in prices would create an expectation of a further fall, or of a recovery! Unfortunately, no such "pure psychology" exists in a form useful to economics. Even if it did, the economist would need to know only its conclusions. He would not need to know the mechanism by which stimuli evoke responses, provided that he knew what responses would be made to the stimuli which concern him. He would not need to know the exact nature or seat of emotions, if he knew that certain situations arouse emotions influencing economic behaviour in a definite manner, just as he need only know that a hungry man wants food, and need not study the physiology of rhythmic contractions of the stomach.

It is also evident that the economist studies things which do not interest the psychologist. The psychologist, having discussed the "wish for prestige", does not proceed to explain the price discrepancy between bread and diamonds. Having analysed the bases of ethnocentrism, he does not elucidate the conditions for mutually advantageous trade between two countries. Economics and psychology are related but quite distinct sciences. To put it briefly and a trifle incautiously, what are for psychologists "effects" are for economists "causes". The psychologist considers his task finished when he has discovered and explained the tendencies of human behaviour. The economist takes these tendencies as given, along with technological data, and proceeds to analyse the production and distribution of goods and services.

Psychologists have shown one thing of real significance for economic theory; the danger of introspective analysis.[9] Economists now recognize that merely asking "What do I do?" or "What do you do?" is not enough. They are exceedingly cautious in their *explanations* of economic choices. They no longer speak of choices being determined by "utility", in the sense of estimated satisfaction. Any assumptions about economic behaviour that are left standing in the final analysis are derived from *observation*. They are of a sort that can be obtained from every-day experience, and which are independent of *any* psychological theories. The "law of diminishing elasticity of substitution", which underlies the modern theory of value, is of this sort. The empirical fact that people do not spend all their income on one commodity provides general support for it, while family budget studies, laboratory experiments, and statistical studies provide more detailed verification. Economics is based on psychology, but it is psychology of a very simple sort, consisting of generalizations that are either axiomatic or easily derived from observation of every-day behaviour.

The Method of Economics

Popular confusion regarding the nature of knowledge in economics arises naturally from a failure to understand the method of economics, and to recognize the fundamental similarity of the methodology of economics and of other sciences.[10] In broad outline, the method of economics is the "scientific method" outlined by Aristotle, and followed by virtually all scientists ever since. It begins with observations; it next deduces general laws from these observations; finally,

9 Cf. B. Higgins, "A Note on the Relationship of Psychology to Economics" (*The Manchester School*, May 1935); and "The Economic Man and Economic Science" (*Canadian Journal of Economics and Political Science*, November 1947).

10 Misunderstanding of the method of economics appears to exist even among distinguished representatives of related social sciences. D. W. Brogan, Professor of Political Science at the University of Cambridge, has said recently in a review of *Science and Politics*, by A. D. Ritchie, that:

"Primitive as it is, social science is not as primitive as it was. In its methodology it is not like physics or even the biological sciences, and its results are less certain, less general, less permanent. But into the study of human affairs something of the spirit of the exact sciences has been imported, and one fairly well established result has been the understanding

it tests these generalizations empirically. Laymen and elementary students are often misled by the obvious nature of some of the original observations. The simple facts that virtually no one spends all his income on a single commodity, and that commodities can be produced with varying proportions of land, labour, and capital, enable the economist to go an astonishingly long way in the second, or deductive, stage of analysis. The large amount of space devoted to this stage in economic literature, particularly in textbooks on "principles", has given the impression that economics is a good deal more deductive than it really is. The basic observations are there, but sometimes they are so axiomatic as to need no explicit statement.

Within the deductive stage, the method of "successive approximations" is used. That is, the analyst begins with a model that is deliberately simplified, to isolate a particular relationship and so make analysis possible. Complications of the real world are removed by assumption, and then re-introduced one by one; at each step, conclusions are modified in whatever manner is logically necessary. This process is the economist's substitute for physical experiments; it is only the simplest kinds of elementary observation that permit laboratory experiment under control, and the use of statistics is limited by scarcity of reliable and comparable data. Consequently, the economist is compelled to rely in large measure on what the Austrians have called "Gedanken-experimenten" or "logical experiments".

Empirical testing, however, has been a major part of the economist's interest, especially in recent years; unfortunately, this testing necessarily takes one of three forms: economic history, which the layman tends to regard as something different from economics proper; statistics, which the layman dismisses as dull; or econometrics, which many laymen (and

of the great differences which there must be between the exact sciences and the would-be sciences of social organization and human behaviour. The acceptance of as much of the spirit of the exact sciences as human frailty and the character of the materials permits, the acceptance of the ideas that an exact, infallible, quasi-mathematical science of society is impossible, these results are not everything, but they are something" (*Nature*, Jan. 1948, p. 7).

Professor Brogan would have done better to have used the term "political science" in this passage, rather than "social science".

not a few economists) find incomprehensible because of the mathematics involved. Economic analysis, and economic laws, are essentially mathematical in form, even when no mathematics are actually used, because economic analysis and laws are concerned with the effects of small changes in one variable upon the values of other variables in the system. Mathematics tend to arouse the awe and admiration of the layman when used in other sciences, but often lead to suspicion when used in economics.[11] For these reasons, the layman is often unaware of the great extent to which economics is an empirical science.

Economic Laws

By the use of this method, economists have been able to develop three kinds of economic laws: *a priori* laws, deduced laws, and empirical laws.[12] A simple example of an *a priori* law is the Fisher equation of exchange, $MV = PT$ (M is the volume of money, V the velocity of circulation of money, P the general price level, and T the "number of transactions", or the volume of goods and services sold, during an income period). If the quantities are properly defined, this law cannot possibly be wrong. It states the obvious fact that the quantity of money spent on goods and services in a given period is equal to the quantity of money received from sales of goods and services in the same period. Yet such a law can be extraordinarily useful. For example, it can be rewritten $P = MV/T$, which tells us that in a period of full employ-

---

11 I was once attacked by the editor of the Canadian *Chartered Accountant* for using equations in an article on tax policy, published by the *Canadian Journal of Economics and Political Science,* a professional journal. The editor felt that the use of equations necessarily implied a degree of rigidity of human behaviour that could only be achieved in a totalitarian state, and that some kind of revolutionary plot was hidden behind my symbols.

12 The distinction is slightly artificial, because deduced laws may have an *a priori* basis, and may be empirically verified. Immanuel Kant defines *a priori* laws as follows: "Experience teaches us that a thing is so and so, but not that it cannot be otherwise. . . . Experience never confers on its judgments true or strict, but only assumed and comparative universality, through induction. We can properly only say, therefore, that, so far as we have hitherto observed, there is no exception to this or that rule. If, then, a judgment is thought with strict universality, that is in such a manner that no exception is allowed as possible, it is not derived from experience but is valid absolutely *a priori*" (*Critique of Pure Reason,* edited and translated by Norman Kemp Smith, London, 1939, pp. 43-44).

ment, when the total supply of goods and services cannot be quickly increased, a rapid increase in the volume of money will cause inflation unless something is done to reduce the velocity of circulation of money — by, say, taxing or borrowing people's money away and then holding it idle. A still more useful law of the same type states that the change in income from the last income period to the present one is equal to (planned investment less planned savings) plus (government expenditures on goods and services less tax collections) plus (exports less imports), all in the present period. This law tells us, for example, that inflation can be checked, but only in a limited number of ways: by restricting private investment and encouraging savings; reducing government expenditures and raising taxes; reducing exports and increasing imports. It also tells us that unemployment can be cured by the reverse policies, and only by those policies.

Certain additional laws can be deduced from *a priori* propositions. Most of the theory of taxation consists of such laws. For example, if we assume that a monopolist runs his firm so as continuously to maximize profits, we can deduce that he will restrict his output to the level at which one more unit would add more to total costs than it would to total receipts. It can then be further shown that a lump sum or percentage tax on the monopolist's profits cannot be "shifted"; i.e., it will not pay the entrepreneur to raise his price and reduce his sales and output further. If then we introduce into the model the monopolist's desire for leisure, we can deduce that the tax on monopoly profits will be partially shifted; and so on.

An example of an empirical law is the consumption function, that is to say, the relationship between consumers' spending and changes in the level and distribution of national income. One version of this law for the American economy has been provided by Dr. Lawrence Klein:[13]

$$C = 16 \cdot 78 + \cdot 02\,P + \cdot 23\,P_- + \cdot 80\,(W_1 + W_2) + U^1_1$$

[13] Lawrence R. Klein, *Economic Fluctuations in the United States 1921-1941*, (New York, Wiley, 1950), p. 68.

He also provides an investment function:[14]

$$I = 17·79_4^1 + 23_a^1 P + ·55 P_{-1} - ·15 K_{-1} + U^1{}_2$$

In the past decade or two, a good deal of the effort of economists has been devoted to "econometrics", which is concerned with the discovery of such empirical laws. A beginning has been made at building statistical "models" of particular economies, consisting of sets of simultaneous equations, which together describe (and in that limited sense "explain") the operation of an entire economy, in terms of such significant aggregates as the level of national income, consumer spending, investment, prices, and the distribution of income between wages and profits.

Knowledge in Economics and in Physics

The layman, however, is not much concerned with the scope and method of economics, nor with a classification of economic laws. What he wants to know is, "Will the laws work?" In answering this question, it may be instructive to compare the laws of economics with the laws of some science which the layman considers completely trustworthy. Among the so-called "exact" sciences, physics appears to command most general respect. How do the laws of economics compare with the laws of physics?

There can be no difference in exactness between the *a priori* laws of physics and economics. All *a priori* laws are one hundred per cent exact by definition. The worst that can be said of them is that they are sometimes of limited use for prognosis and prescription in particular times and places. In the Fisher equation cited above, for example, the actual effect on the price level of doubling the quantity of money cannot be predicted, without knowledge of the precise quantitative relationships between M, V, and T. Such strictures apply equally to *a priori* laws in physics. Laws stating that the whole is greater than its parts, other Euclidean laws, or the hydrodynamic law that the flow of an incompressible

---

14 In these equations, C is consumption, I is investment, P is profits, W_1 is wages of non-governmental employees, W_2 is wages of governmental employees, K is the stock of capital, $U^1{}_1$ and $U^1{}_2$ are "disturbances", which may include the effects of trends. The subscripts refer to income periods.

fluid is identical for each of its cross-sections, are *in themselves* of limited use to engineers. Of course, the designer of bridges, having more useful empirical laws, does not have to rely on *a priori* laws to the same extent as the designer of monetary policies; but in so far as *a priori* laws are used, they are all equally true, whatever the field of knowledge.

The deduced laws of economics often involve a high degree of abstraction from reality. So do the deduced laws of physics. No man has a brain powerful enough to comprehend the universe, merely by seeing it steadily and seeing it whole. To isolate causal relationships, any scientist must concentrate on a tiny segment of the universe, deliberately protected from the effects of other relationships present in the real world.[15] If Newton had been content to sit under apple trees while apples dropped on his head, birds soared above, leaves whirled in the wind, and boys flew kites, he would never have isolated the law of velocity of falling bodies. To determine this law, it was necessary for him to consider bodies falling in a vacuum, from which the effects of atmospheric pressure, air currents, temperature changes and the like were deliberately abstracted. Heroic simplifications are also made in the mathematical models of theoretical physics.[16]

Nor could an engineer develop an accurate bomb-sight by

---

[15] "Let us assume", begins Dr. W. D. MacMillan in discussing the motion of the centre of gravity of an isolated system, "a system that is isolated (with) . . . no exterior forces acting, or exterior forces so small as to be negligible". He then appeals to established (Newtonian) laws of motion, and deduces mathematically the equation $T - T_0 = W^{(1)} + W^{(e)}$, where T is kinetic energy, T_0 is kinetic energy at a previous point of time, $W^{(1)}$ is the work done by interior forces, and $W^{(e)}$ the work done by exterior forces. How like economics it all sounds! (See W. D. MacMillan, *Dynamics of Rigid Bodies*, New York and London 1936, pp. 59-65). Deduction on principles valid only in simplified systems is common practice among physicists. One more example: H. O. Newboult (*Analytical Method in Dynamics*, Oxford, 1946, p. 1) *deduces* that Newton's second-law of dynamics is valid in a system where the direction is fixed and the origin has no acceleration.

[16] Max Planck, discoverer of the quantum theory that revolutionized modern physics, writes in this regard: "This alternative play of theory and experiment, of theoretical constructions on the side of abstract reason and the testing of these by their application to objective reality, is a special characteristic of modern physics. Indeed, it is of enormous significance in all scientific progress, for it is the one safe and sound source from which reliable and enduring results can be produced" (*Where is Science Going?*, New York, 1932, p. 45).

working with the law of gravity alone. All relevant forces, from which deliberate abstraction is made to obtain a law of gravity, must be reintroduced at the point of application to particular problems. The same is true of the deduced laws of economics. So long as the model within which laws are developed is one which leaves out of account pertinent factors of the real world, the laws cannot be applied to real problems. However, their inadequacy for the solution of particular problems does not make them *wrong*, any more than the law of gravity is wrong because it is an inadequate basis for designing an aeroplane.

There is one important difference between the generalizations that the economist deduces from his initial observations and the generalizations of the physicist. That difference, however, redounds to the credit of the economist rather than the physicist. Precisely because of his limited physical control over strategic variables, the economist tends to insist on explanations which are *both* necessary and sufficient, and is extremely wary of merely sufficient explanations.[17] He is all too keenly aware of pitfalls in the form of extremely high "nonsense correlation" coefficients. When, for example, he discovered an extremely high correlation between the regional variations in Swedish birth rates and the regional distribution of storks, he did not leap to the simple conclusion that storks bring the babies, nor yet to the equally plausible conclusion that babies bring storks. He asked himself, "Is it *logically necessary* that babies *must* be brought by storks, or is there some conceivable way in which babies could arrive without the storks, and storks arrive without babies?"

---

[17] The natural scientist, especially if he is an experimental rather than a theoretical scientist, is sometimes suspicious of the "logical experiments", by which the deduced laws of economics are derived. One cannot help feeling, however, that the reason for this suspicion is that not all natural scientists are trained to *think* clearly. Their universe is relatively uncomplicated, and they can make their abstractions physically; consequently, they can make a good deal of progress by mere "pointer-reading", which does not require much abstract *thinking*. Even the use of higher mathematics is not quite the same as clear thinking: the use of mathematics is an *aid* to clear thinking and a check to muddled thinking, but knowledge of higher mathematics is no substitute for logical analysis. This kind of confusion is even more common among engineers and other technicians.

The physicist, on the other hand, is prone to accept merely sufficient explanations of his observations, without insisting that these explanations be *logically necessary,* as well as fitting the facts.[18] Some of the generalizations that have been widely accepted by physicists seem to the layman only slightly less näive than an explanation of variations of Swedish birth rates in terms of movements of storks. Examples are the nineteenth century theory that heat is due to the action of an elastic and self-repellent fluid, or the "action at a distance" theory of magnetism. Another example is provided by the various ether theories, especially the endeavours to make the ether theory compatible with Maxwell's equations for electro magnetism, which "explained" magnetism as layers of idle and rotating particles.

As J. W. N. Sullivan puts it:[19]

On the whole, the theory of the ether represents one of the most laborious and least satisfactory expenditures of ingenuity in the history of science. No ether was constructed by mathematicians that fulfilled all the demands made on it. As the ether became more complicated it became more unplausible and unaesthetic. Space became filled with an incredible combination of cogwheels, gyroscopes and driving bands. It resembled nothing so much as the nightmare of some mad engineer. . . . Suppose, for instance, that an ether model consisting of wheels, each wheel geared to four neighbours by india rubber bands, the bands being of varying elasticity and also capable of slipping, suppose that such a model is shown to be capable of transmitting vibrations analagous to those of light, what precisely is proved?

Now, as I understand it, the nineteenth-century theories of heat and magnetism, and most of the ether theories, have turned out to be just plain wrong. The fact that physicists have accepted so many wrong theories, containing errors that even their mathematics did not detect until new data necessitated a change in their fundamental equations, can be

---

18 Professor Susan Stebbing points out: "The concepts in terms of which Newton gave his description of phenomena have been replaced by a different set. That mere fact shows that his concepts were not *necessary* concepts". Jevons' "sunspot theory" of business cycles was a "sufficient" explanation, but just for that reason it was never accepted by anyone but Jevons himself, and later by J. L. Moore.

19 J. W. N. Sullivan, *The Bases of Modern Science,* London 1928, Chapter III (p. 51 of Pelican edition).

traced directly to the contentment of physicists with merely sufficient explanations.[20]

The economist, on the other hand, is chary of accepting any theory that could possibly be proved wrong by new empirical discoveries. For this reason, and because great economists have necessarily been good logicians, generally accepted economic laws have seldom been completely wrong. Theories have been shown to be incomplete, and have been replaced by theories of greater generality, just as the classical system of physics has been expanded by later discoveries without its fundamental principles being disproved. The history of economic thought, as well as the method of the deductive stage of economics, is one of successive approximations to reality. For example, the labour theory of value, accepted by the classical economists, of the late eighteenth and early nineteenth centuries, was not *wrong,* in the sense that the theory of continuity of radiation was wrong; it was only *incomplete,* in the same way that the law of gravity is an incomplete explanation of the path of a projectile. Within the classical framework of pure competition and constant costs, it is perfectly true that "given demand, prices in equilibrium will vary proportionately to

---

20 One source of misunderstanding between economists and natural scientists is the different use of the term "theory". The physicist usually means by "theory" an hypothesis or tentative explanation of observed phenomena, as distinct from a "law". The economist, on the other hand, uses "theory" and "law" almost as synonyms. The "theory of price", for example, does not mean merely an hypothesis about price determination, but the collection of laws (such as they are) of price determination. For this reason, the economist may not recognize at once that physical *theories* can be proved wrong without destroying the validity of the physical *laws* to which the theories were attached. Thus Professor Brown writes:

"Contrary to certain popular notions, nothing in modern physics contradicts or sets aside any of the facts or laws of the older physics, within the range of experience for which they have been found valid. Whenever new concepts appear to be at variance with earlier ideas, the disagreements are with *extrapolations* of the earlier laws and concepts, beyond the range of experience for which they were established. Now a good scientist never assumes that any extrapolations of the laws of science are valid until they have been tested by experiment. Nor does he carry out explorations in new regions for the purpose of *proving* the validity of any extrapolations. It is a fundamental principle of science to search for the truth, then to make laws which fit the discoveries. If the extrapolations do not fit the new experiments, new laws are required, although the old laws remain valid over the range of experience for which they were originally established" (Thomas B. Brown, *Foundations of Modern Physics,* New York and London 1949, p. 2) .

differences in labour cost of production" (including in labour-costs the labour embodied in capital goods, and remembering that under the conditions assumed only "normal" profits can be earned). It is now recognized that the classical case is a special one; pure competition is the exception rather than the rule, and costs are seldom constant over the entire relevant range of output. In cases of monopoly, or in cases where cost-per-unit varies with the level of output, the labour theory is inadequate as an explanation of differences in prices. But even in such cases, the (direct and indirect) labour cost of production is a major factor in the determination of price.[21]

The theory of demand, and the theory of maximization of "ophelimity" (total satisfaction, or "utility") that underlies it, has been subject to more outside criticism on methodological grounds than any other branch of economics. Recently, however, several writers have noticed the close analogy between "ophelimity" and the concept of "entropy" in thermo-dynamics.[22] Ophelimity is a logarithmic function of the stock of commodities, just as entropy is a logarithmic function of the stock of energy. Marginal utility in economics corresponds to the (reciprocal of the) intensity factor in thermo-dynamics. The economic subject maximizes ophelimity, by equating marginal utilities. Nature maximizes entropy by equating final temperatures, or intensity factors. It is interesting to note also that heat, like ophelimity, can-

[21] The history of physics, too, might be regarded as a process of successive approximations to reality. Professor Brown points out:

"In most cases, indeed, these newer laws are valid over the entire range of experience, such that the older ones must be considered as approximations to the newer. This does not, however, discredit the older laws. Within the range for which they were originally established they still are valid, and generally more convenient to use than the newer ones. Many examples of this may be found, even in the older parts of physics. Thus the 'rays' of geometrical optics are only approximations to the paths followed by light waves, but they provide the easiest way to solve many optical problems. Boyle's law is another example. This law has definite limitations (see Sec. 156) but is always used when these limitations are not exceeded" (op. cit., p. 2).

[22] See for example J. S. Lisman, "Econometrics and Thermo-dynamics", Econometrica, January 1949; H. T. Davis, The Theory of Econometrics, Bloomington, Indiana 1941, esp. pp. 174-181; A. Pinkler, "Die dynamischen Geldtheorien und die mechanischen Analogien", Volkswirthschaftliche Rundschen (Budapest), Nos. 1 and 2, 1933.

not be measured cardinally and absolutely, but only relatively and ordinally. A thermometer doesn't register heat, but the expansion of mercury, hydrogen, or helium as a reaction to heat. It would be perfectly possible to develop an "ophelometer" along the same lines.[23] It is also worth noting that "ophelimity" is not a mere invention of the economist, conceived by him to provide a sufficient explanation of variations in prices, but has real content and is discernible in individual behaviour.

The empirical laws of economics, like those of physics, are statistical laws. They state that certain aggregative relationships have been observed in the past, and that there is a high degree of probability that these relationships will continue in the future. True, the probability coefficients attached to the statistical laws of economics are considerably lower than those attached to the statistical laws of physics. Physical laws that are 99.99 per cent probable are not uncommon; while economists are pleased to discover empirical laws that are only 90 per cent certain. The empirical laws of economics are probably more subject to improvement and refinement as more data become available. For example, it may develop that a trend factor in a consumption function is not a constant, but a function of time. Thus economic statistical laws may become "truer" as knowledge accumulates. Methodologically, however, the statistical laws of physics and economics are fundamentally the same sort of thing.

In one respect, indeed, the statistical laws of economics are even more "scientific" than some of the statistical laws in physics. In both sciences, aggregative laws applied to large numbers of individuals are more precise than laws applied to single individuals. The economist, however, is always reluctant to accept an aggregative law unless it is plausible in terms of the laws applying to individual households and firms. The physicist, on the other hand, accepts statistical laws providing their statistical probability is high enough, even if he is unable to deduce the aggregative law from his

---

[23] Cf. Roy Harrod, *Towards a Dynamic Economics*, London 1948, pp. 43-4.

knowledge of the behaviour of individual particles, such as electrons. The difference can be illustrated by suggesting that the statistical laws of economics resemble those of behaviour of gases, rather than the laws of radiation. Professor Stebbing summarizes the difference between these laws as follows:[24]

A gas is composed of a vast number of molecules moving very rapidly in all directions, constantly colliding with one another and altering their directions. It is not in practice possible to determine the velocity or the path of an individual molecule. All that can be done is to say what is the average velocity, and what path, on the average, is followed between one collision and the next. It is, however, assumed that the movement of each molecule, that is, its velocity and path, does in fact take place in accordance with definite laws; in short, that the movement is causally determined. Thus, although only statistical laws can be applied, it is held that these laws are based upon causal laws. It is assumed that it is not absurd to suppose that, could we ascertain the initial conditions of a molecule's movement, we could predict where exactly it would be at a later moment. . . The case is otherwise with the electron jumps of Bohr's theory. There is no way of discovering when an electron will jump, nor to which orbit it will jump. The initial state does not determine the final state; hence, the final state is unpredictable.

When the economist relies on statistical laws, he does not do so because the behaviour of an individual household or firm is intrinsically unpredictable, but because the behaviour of individual households and firms is not completely known, just as the behaviour of individual gas molecules is not completely known. The economist does not exclude the possibility that as the social sciences advance, the behaviour of individual households and firms may some day be predictable with a high degree of accuracy.[25] Indeed, the economist

24 Susan Stebbing, *op. cit.*, pp. 135-6.
25 It is interesting to note that Max Planck does exclude this possibility either. With regard to human behaviour he has the following to say:

"While the historian or the sociologist strives to apply purely objective methods to his lines of investigation, he finds himself confronted on all hands with the want of data whereby he might determine the causes that have led to general conditions in the past and lead to the general conditions in the world at the present moment. At the same time, however, he has at least one advantage here which the physicist has not. The historian or the sociologist is dealing with the same kind of activities as he finds in himself. . . . In psychology we have a definite individual personality to study. That individual personality has inherited qualities such as bodily conformation,

already knows a good deal about the behaviour of his individual particles. The development of economics has been just the reverse of the development of physics in this respect. While the history of modern physics has been a matter of breaking up aggregates into smaller and smaller particles, the economist *began* with his laws of behaviour of individual particles (people), and proceeded to laws regarding the behaviour of the system as a whole.[26] The theory of households and firms still comprises the major portion of most elementary textbooks of economics, and the economist can predict certain kinds of individual behaviour with a high degree of probability. For example, if a household divides its income among thirty commodities, and the price of each of these falls in succession, it is highly probable that the household will increase its consumption of all of them, except those that are available only in very large indivisible units. Similarly, it is highly probable that if a firm suffers a decline in demand for each of ten commodities it produces, it will reduce its output of most of them. Thus a consumption function, which relates in the form of an empirical equation the factors determining the level of aggregative community spending, or an investment function isolating the

intelligence, imaginative capacity, temperament, personal tastes and so on. Working on this personality we have the physical and psychic influences of the environment, such as climate, food, upbringing, companionship, family life, education, reading, etc. Now the question is whether all these data determine the conduct of this personality in all its particulars and according to definite laws. In other words, if we suppose, what is impossible in practice, that we had a thorough and detailed knowledge of all these factors here and now, could we tell with certainty, on the causal basis, how the individual will act a moment hence? . . . I think that it may be said definitely that the direction in which the humanist sciences, such as psychology and history, are developing nowadays furnishes certain grounds for presuming that the question should be answered in the affirmative. The part which force plays in nature, as the cause of motion, has its counterpart in the mental sphere in motive as the cause of conduct. Just as at each and every moment the motion of a material body results necessarily from the combined action of many forces, so human conduct results with the same necessity from the interplay of mutually reinforced or contradicting motives, which partly in the conscious and partially also in the unconscious sphere work their way forward towards the result" (*Where is Science Going?*. pp. 150-153).

[26] This statement applies especially to the development of economics over the past seventy-five years. The approach of the Classical School combined macro- and micro-economics to some extent. Even the Classical School, however, built up its generalizations about the whole system from a theory of individual behaviour.

factors determining the aggregate level of private investment are not *merely* statistical laws; they conform to the theories of behaviour of individual households and firms. While the probability coefficients of the empirical laws of economics are lower than those of physics, methodologically the statistical laws of economics appear to be on more solid ground.

To the layman, however, the value of the probability coefficients attaching to the empirical laws may seem much the most important consideration. The layman wants to know how reliable economic laws are as a basis for policy — for, say, eliminating the dangers of unemployment, inflation, social conflict, revolution and war. Surely, he would interject, the fact that physicists can *predict*, while the economist cannot, is an overwhelmingly important difference between the two sciences?

But what is it that the physicist can predict? Can he predict when an apple will fall, or even when the bulk of all the apples in an orchard will fall? Can he say how long a bridge will last? Can he foretell whether a particular gunshot will sink an enemy ship, or even whether a bomb will totally destroy a factory if it hits it? Faced with such problems, the physicist can only state some probabilities, and in some cases very low ones at that. If he is to predict with the very high degrees of probability attaching to his so-called "exact" laws, the problem must be limited to the model to which his laws apply. The range of problems about which natural scientists can predict with certainty is really very small. Given equal rights and powers to restrict his model, the economist can predict many things with one hundred per cent accuracy. Even in models closely approximating the real world, he can predict a good many things with a high degree of accuracy. The economist's difficulty is that he is usually presented with problems involving factors outside his sphere of special knowledge, and that he is not given the legal powers he would need to limit his model in a manner permitting accurate predictions.[27]

27 Professor Ritchie says: "The rules already formulated (in social science) are generally only assertions of what happens for the most part, not of what

What Economists Do Not Know

I do not wish to give the impression that economists know everything necessary to design a policy to eliminate economic instability and social conflict, let alone revolutions and wars. On the contrary, there are glaring gaps between what economists know and what they need to know to formulate such a policy.

First of all, economists do not know what is "good" for people. In a later lecture, I shall discuss the objectives of economic policy in some detail. At this stage, I should like merely to suggest that the economist has two alternatives with regard to selection of objectives of policy. First, he may accept the objectives handed to him by the community through their democratically elected governments. Secondly, he may make some value judgments of his own. The economist who makes public pronouncements on policy usually bases them on two value judgments: first, that it is "good" for people to be happy; and second, that (other things being equal) people are made happier by having more goods, services and leisure to consume. In other words, he assumes that people know what they want, and that what they want is good for them. On the basis of these judgments, he accepts the maximization of satisfaction through consumption of goods and services as the appropriate objective of economic policy. He can then demonstrate that the achievement of this objective requires full employment without inflation, an optimum allocation of resources among various goods and services, an optimum rate of economic growth, and an optimum distribution of income. He can translate the first two of these objectives into quantitative terms. The third one is more difficult to define quantitatively, but a defensible range

---

happens always: not the stricter ones of physics" (*Science and Politics*). From my very limited knowledge of biology, I would say that the laws of economics resemble "the looser laws of biology" less than almost any other kind of laws. The laws of biology are mainly classificatory, descriptive, and statistical; there are very few *a priori* laws of any significance, and not many deduced laws. Here again, we can't help feeling that Professor Ritchie is describing laws of political science, or possibly sociology, rather than laws of economics. Moreover, few contemporary physicists would be so bold as to assert that physical laws state what "happens always".

of rates of economic growth can be delimited. When he comes to the fourth objective, however, the economist must make a third value judgment. He cannot prove that a pound taken from the millionaire, who has developed sensitive and refined taste, and given to the pauper who has never learned to enjoy life, will add to total satisfaction. Yet nearly all economists *believe* that policies which attain the other objectives in a manner making income distribution more equal are "better" than policies which do so while making income distribution more unequal. All three of these value judgments are plausible, but they cannot be included among the things economists *know*.

In the second place, the economist knows very little about the rules governing the behaviour of such powerful social groups as employers' associations, trade unions, farmers' organizations, and governments. Yet a coal-miners' strike, or the tightening of monopoly control through a trade association, or the withholding of agricultural products from the market by farmers' co-operatives, may considerably alter the economic outlook, while decisions of the United States Congress or the Russian Politburo can totally transform the economic situation. In the past, economists have, with some justice, dismissed such matters as "non-economic". More recently, economists have recognized that since the behaviour of such groups is of overwhelming importance in the production and distribution of goods and services, and because no one else seems to be studying this behaviour in a way calculated to provide answers to economists' questions, economists must interest themselves in such peripheral fields as political science and sociology. Economists must also study group behaviour for themselves, as a legitimate part of economic analysis. What is needed here is an extension of the economists' empirical knowledge, an extension that will require teamwork by economists and representatives of other social scientific disciplines.[28]

---

[28] A quotation or two will illustrate the growing recognition of these facts among economists:

"By combining the relevant results of social psychology, anthropology, law, political science, etc., economic sociology should be established on a

In the third place, there is a great deal that economists do not know for sure about entrepreneurial behaviour—things that must be known in order to predict the results of certain kinds of policy. For example, economists cannot predict the effect of a wage-cut on the level of employment, without knowing whether employers will expect the initial wage-cut to lead to another, whether they will think mainly of the cost-reducing aspects of lower wages or of the reduction in purchasing power, whether smaller payrolls will lead to reduced working balances of firms with the banks, the extent to which reduced interest rates will encourage more investment, and so on. Similarly, the amount of public investment needed to maintain full employment in a downswing will depend partly on the amount of unfavourable reaction by private entrepreneurs to the expansion of government activity. The precise effect of a tax on business profits will depend on the extent to which entrepreneurs' behaviour is dominated by desire to maximize profits and the extent to which it is affected by such rival motives as the wish to play golf, to own a large firm, to outsell competitors, to avoid trouble with the union, and to escape application of anti-trust laws. The theory of behaviour of the firm under conditions of oligopoly reached a *cul de sac,* because economists could not determine to what extent entrepreneurs go through a "he thinks that I think that he thinks that I think" analysis regarding probable reaction of rivals to a change in his price policy: and it is not yet certain that the "theory of games"[29] approach to oligopoly theory will rescue it from this blind alley.

Of course, the economist can make varying assumptions

---

much broader basis and on permanent contact with the progress of economics itself and with its varying questions" (Adolf Lowe, *op. cit.* p. 149) .

" 'The border-lands of economics,' writes Professor Robbins, 'are the happy hunting-ground of the charlatan and the quack.' It will be a pity if they are left in undisputed possession" (L. M. Fraser, "How do we want Economics to Behave?" *Economic Journal,* December 1932) . See also E. F. M. Durbin, "Methods of Research—a Plea for Co-operation in the Social Sciences," *Economic Journal,* June 1938, and J. R. Commons, *The Economics of Collective Action* (New York, 1950) .

29 Morgenstern and Neumann, *The Theory of Games, and Economic Behaviour* (Princeton, 1944) , *passim.*

about these matters and derive precise conclusions on the
basis of these assumptions; this procedure provides a range
of possible results, but does not tell us which results will
occur in a specific case. It is also possible to find out something about the behaviour of entrepreneurs by observing
them in their native habitat.[30] Even expectations are not
unknowable. Expectations are facts, like any other facts—only
they are difficult to ascertain.[31] Unfortunately, the attitude of
entrepreneurs to wage cuts, is not a law in the sense that
maximization of ophelimity is a law. Attitude towards wage
cuts can change. Sometimes the economist finds himself
wondering whether he will ever catch up with his changing
universe! The problem is still further complicated by the
fact that the conclusions and forecasts of economists themselves effect economic developments.[32]

Conclusions

In sum, economics is less of a science than physics, in terms
of the number of thoroughly established and applicable

---

[30] It may be necessary, however, to observe them from behind a one-way
screen; knowledge that they are under scrutiny tends to influence their
behaviour!

[31] Cf. F. A. v. Hayek, *Individualism and the Economic Order*, London 1949,
Ch. III.

[32] At that, it is at least debatable whether the economist is worse off than the
physicist in this regard. In the first place, certain observations in physics
affect the behaviour of the particles under observation; "In the world of
very small dimensions the observation is not independent of the observer"
(Carl Trueblood Chase, *The Evolution of Modern Physics*, New York 1947,
p. 181). No "unit" smaller than a human being is capable of human
behaviour. The economist therefore has the great advantage of being able to
see his "particles". The physicist, on the other hand, must rely a good deal
on *indirect* evidence:

"The earlier physics boasted of being an experimental science, and, for
the most part, it consisted of fairly direct generalizations derived from
experimental data. We may say that the experimental data provided *direct
evidence* to establish and support the laws of this earlier part of physics.
The physical existence of the entities of this earlier physics was unquestioned
because those entities were directly observable. Modern physics also boasts
of being an experimental science, but the entities with which it is most
concerned are, with few exceptions, hopelessly invisible. For the most part,
the experimental data from which all our knowledge concerning atoms,
electrons, photons, and the like is derived, provide *indirect or circumstantial
evidence*, rather than direct evidence. This in no wise invalidates the
deductions from such data. Circumstantial evidence can be the most reliable
kind of evidence provided there is enough of it and observers know how to
interpret it" (Thomas B. Brown, *op. cit.*, p. 3).

laws it has accumulated; but economics is perhaps more *scientific,* in the sense that its *method* is better calculated to distinguish the true from the untrue. If economics is less exact than the natural sciences, it is at the same time more exacting.

Concretely, economists know enough to explain reasonably well how firms determine their prices and output, how national income is distributed among households, how households allocate their income among various goods and services (including imports) and how the general level of income, employment, and prices is determined. Economists cannot predict actual economic conditions very far into the future, because they know too little about the expectations of entrepreneurs, and about the behaviour of governments, trade unions, employers' associations and farmers' organizations; so far, economists have made only limited progress with the theory of general economic development. For these reasons, economists cannot predict with certainty the results of every kind of policy measure. What precisely does all that add up to, with regard to the economist's ability to solve economic problems?

The situation is not as bad as might appear at first sight. Specific objectives of economic policy can usually be obtained by measures which can be shown to be effective with a high degree of certainty; one need seldom resort to more dubious measures. Wage cuts, for example, are a very clumsy device for promoting recovery as compared to fiscal policy, and the uncertainty of the effects of wage cuts is consequently of little practical importance. Uncertainty as to how a particular entrepreneur will behave is not very serious, because few policy measures apply only to single entrepreneurs; and aggregate laws are relatively exact, because they allow for offsetting abberations of individual entrepreneurs. For example, if some entrepreneurs prefer more leisure to more profits, while others prefer running a big show to higher profits gained through restricting sales and raising prices, entrepreneurs *as a group* will behave much as though they all sought to maximize profits.

At worst, the economist can usually demonstrate that the

alternative policy suggestions of the layman would not work at all; and it is obviously better to adopt a policy with an 80 : 20 chance of success — or even 60 : 40 — than one that has no chance whatsoever of succeeding.

Even with present knowledge, a team of economists — selected, let us say, by the membership of the Royal Economic Society — and provided with unlimited *legal* powers, could maintain full employment without inflation; could produce a close approximation to an optimum allocation of resources and a fair approximation to an optimal rate of economic progress; and it could improve the income distribution at the same time. Over the course of a century, a series of such teams could devise policies that would maintain an average level of national real income substantially higher than could be achieved under *laisser-faire,* and considerably higher than could be achieved by planners with identical legal powers but no training in economics. Eliminating unemployment might add twenty-five per cent to national real income. In most countries, the average loss through unemployment during the interwar period was less than this amount; but in the absence of appropriate policies, economic fluctuations are likely to increase in amplitude, and to take place around a trend involving an increasing amount of chronic under-employment. Eliminating the misallocation of resources resulting from monopoly and inflation might add another twenty or twenty-five per cent to national real income, and preventing the waste of resources by short-sighted individual planners (who tend to "mine" soil and forest) would add something more.

Altogether, a team of competent economists with ample legal powers might succeed in producing an average level of real national income fifty per cent higher than would occur under *laissez-faire,* or thirty per cent higher than could be produced by any group of non-economists with the same powers. In any country in the world, increasing the real income of every man, woman, and child by fifty per cent — or even thirty per cent — would be enormously worth while. If income were more equitably distributed in the process, the incomes of the lower income groups could of course be raised by somewhat more than these percentages. But two questions immediately arise. First, what are the chances that a series of teams of economists could agree on national policy? The next lecture deals with this question. Second, just what powers would these experts need? After all, one can pay too high a price in freedom for a higher real income. Many people would bitterly resent being pushed around by experts, no matter how wise and benevolent. I would agree with them. Can economic efficiency be reconciled with freedom from being pushed around? This question is discussed in the last four lectures.

II

ECONOMISTS NEVER AGREE

EVERYONE HAS ENCOUNTERED, in one version or another, the remark which I heard attributed to Winston Churchill: "Whenever I ask England's six leading economists a question, I get seven answers — two from Mr. Keynes." The remark is indicative of the wide-spread impression that "economists never agree", and that the layman might just as well make up his mind on matters of economic policy by himself, without consulting professional economists. In my opening lecture, on the other hand, I spoke of "economists" and "the economist", as though all economists thought alike on every economic issue. It would appear off-hand that there is a wide gulf between the layman's view of the extent of agreement among economists, and the view implicit in my discussion of what economists know. What is the truth of the matter? Considering the gravity of the economic problems with which we are faced today, it is of the utmost importance that the general public should understand the nature and extent of disagreement among professional economists, so that they may distinguish between the questions on which economists can render expert opinions and those on which they cannot.

The Area of Agreement

To convince oneself that economists agree on a great deal, one need only glance through the textbooks on principles of economics that have been published since the war. It is readily apparent that the principles on which economists agree fill hundreds of pages. The economic "facts" which all economists accept would fill thousands of pages. Still more striking is the very wide area of agreement on matters of policy. During the war, the governments of the United States, the United Kingdom, Sweden, Switzerland, Belgium, Canada and Australia invited economists to prepare post-war plans. The political complexion of these governments ranged from Conservative to Social Democratic or Labour. Yet in broad outline the programmes submitted by the economists, and given some degree of official approval by the governments, are strikingly similar. The notable success of the Australian, Canadian, United Kingdom, and United States policies for fighting a total war without serious inflation can be traced to a markedly uniform system of measures, developed by economists of varying political affiliations in these four countries. The replies of the member governments to the United Nations' questionnaire on current full employment policies show strong similarities.

There are, however, three kinds of disagreement among economists. First, they disagree on matters outside the field of economics proper, such as politics and ethics. Second, they disagree on certain details of method. Third, they disagree about certain questions on the frontiers of knowledge in the field of economics proper. For example, there is disagreement among economists regarding the effectiveness of interest rates as an instrument of economic policy; that is, there is uncertainty as to the importance of interest rates in investment decisions, and various economists assess differently the implications of our incomplete knowledge on this subject.

This last sort of disagreement is highly desirable. Controversy about new and unsettled issues of fact and theory is a healthy activity in any scientific field. Disagreement on new discoveries exists in every field of science, including those commonly regarded as most exact. A perusal of recent literature in the field of physics might lead one to believe that "physicists never agree" either. For example, the development of the photon theory by Millikan, Compton, Raman and others has led to renewed controversy as to whether light consists of waves or corpuscles. Even today the wave theory of radiation is still applied in geometric optics, while the corpuscular interpretation is applied in other fields.[1] Not so very long ago, physicists were arguing as to whether the classical laws of dynamics or the Rutherford theory of atomic structure were right. The classical system had proved its usefulness in explaining a wide range of phenomena for many generations, but Rutherford's atom

---

[1] Cf. Carl T. Chase, *The Evolution of Modern Physics*, New York 1947, Ch. 16.

model was the only one that could "meet the experimental results and satisfy the demands of the mathematician".[2] Yet if both theories were right, the universe should have disintegrated long ago! The reconciliation of these two theories was provided by Planck's quantum theory, as elaborated by Bohr and Einstein. At first Planck's theory was "criticized, attacked, and even ridiculed. But it proved brilliantly successful, and ultimately developed into the modern 'quantum theory' which forms one of the dominating principles of modern physics".[3] Thus controversy led to new knowledge. Indeed, the whole history of science could be treated as disagreement leading to discovery. At the end of the eighteenth century, for example, Galvani and Volta disagreed about the nature of electricity. Their disagreement led to sustained controversy, new postulates, and experiment, leading through Faraday's "lines of force" and Maxwell's equations to the modern theory of electro-magnetism. The road to truth is strewn with disagreements.

Professor Gambs compares the extent of disagreement in economics and in the natural sciences in striking fashion:[4]

Imagine an intelligent outlander with no knowledge of Western economics or physics — perhaps Montesquieu's Usbek; give him representative books on economics, published in the past few years, and on the physical sciences. He will come to an interesting conclusion: that economists know exactly what they are doing, because their science is old and mature, their methods well-tested, reliable, and simple. Physics, chemistry and astronomy, on the other hand, being new sciences, just emancipated from superstition, are in a chaotic and yeasty state; the practitioners of those mysteries are even ignorant about what is matter and what is energy — one, Mr. Eddington, having invented the inelegant word "wavicle", to express his acknowledged confusion over waves of energy and particles of matter, while another, Mr. Darwin, awkwardly speaks of electrons as being "matter and/or energy". The physicists invoke Plato, Kant, Hegel, Aristotle, and even Comte and Marx to explain what they are trying to do, while they use such words as dialectic, determinism, causality, absolute, like confirmed metaphysicians — and they

---

2 J. W. N. Sullivan, *The Bases of Modern Science*, London 1928, Ch. VIII.
3 Sir James Jeans, *This Mysterious Universe*, London 1932, p. 19.
4 John S. Gambs, *Beyond Supply and Demand*, New York 1946, p. 84.

use "animism" and "teleology" as often as Veblen did. They have been asking themselves such questions as: Why did human beings so long accept without wonder the fact that glass is transparent? Do I really know what time it is — or, at least, what time it is not? Is the law of gravity a law, or is it a manifestation of man's propensity to put himself at the center of the universe?

Perhaps Professor Gambs goes too far in suggesting that there is more disagreement on fundamental principles among physicists than there is among economists. But he is certainly right in suggesting that some disagreement is necessary to progress in *any* field of knowledge. Vigorous controversy about *new* theories should enhance, rather than destroy, public confidence in economists.

Disagreement of this kind provides no basis for dividing contemporary economists into "schools". If we want to pin labels on economists that will mean anything at all, we must make our classification in terms of methodological and political controversies.

Marxists, Keynesians, Institutionalists, and the "School of Latter-day Laissez-faire"

By stretching a point here and there, it would be possible to divide contemporary economists among four schools: Marxists, Keynesians, Institutionalists, and economists clinging to the neo-classical tradition, and who might be described as "the School of Latter-day Laissez-faire". However, deciding where to put particular economists would not be easy. How, for example, would one classify an economist like Pigou, who uses neo-classical tools, but is a socialist? Or Schumpeter, who uses Marxist tools but is an anti-socialist? And Keynes— surely one of the most original and most articulate of the Keynesians — never lost his faith in the neo-classical principles on which he was raised, and spent much of his time and energy describing the operations of institutions. The best economists combine the best ideas of all four schools, selecting the tools most efficient for the task at hand, whichever "school" may have been responsible for their manufacture. It is only extremists who fall clearly into one category or the other. Accordingly, in my opening lecture the term "economist" was used — I think quite properly — to mean someone combining the wisdom of all four schools. Any division of economists into schools is bound to be somewhat artificial. Nevertheless, the nature and extent of disagreement among economists can be more clearly drawn by considering the differences among idealized versions of these four schools, even if most leading economists would resist classification under any of the four headings.

Methodological Controversies

Let us first consider the methodological differences among these four schools. The neo-classical school, like all economists, uses the "Aristotelian" scientific method. However, it has confined its attention largely to the second, or deductive, stage of analysis. Its preliminary observations have been confined mainly to a few axiomatic facts about economic behaviour, and they have done little empirical testing of their theories. They have tried to develop statistical supply and demand curves, but their efforts merely confirmed ideas about the general shapes of these curves; they did not produce quantitative empirical laws having any degree of reliability. Most of the empirical research done by this school has consisted of description and history, rather than the isolation of empirical functions.

Within the deductive stage, the method of the neo-classicist takes the form of "psychological individualism". Economic behaviour is isolated from other kinds of behaviour for analytical purposes. The individual is assumed to "maximize" something, usually profits or "ophelimity", in relationships involving the production and distribution of goods and services. The analysis is almost entirely "micro-economic"; that is, it is concerned with the behaviour of *individuals,* as consumers, workers, land-owners, investors and entrepreneurs. It is assumed, sometimes without very careful examination of the facts, that the behaviour of the economy as a whole will be a simple summation of the behaviour of individual households and firms; in other words, it is assumed that macro-economics will conform to micro-economics, without direct examination of the aggregative relationships.

The range of inquiry of the neo-classical school has been restricted to statics and comparative statics. That is, they have analysed the forces determining the equilibrium positions of households and firms (and implicitly of the economy as a whole) and the factors leading to a movement from one equilibrium position to another. True, neo-classicists have developed theories of economic fluctuations, but these theories really boil down to micro-economic comparative statics; that is, they have been cast in terms of changes in the equilibrium positions of individual investors, consumers, and entrepreneurs. Indeed, the trade cycle theories of the neo-classicists have been mainly a restatement of equilibrium theories of households and firms, with a few institutional assumptions regarding lags and frictions introduced into the analysis. Dynamics proper — that is, analysis of the development of the system as a whole, or theories of trend — was left to economic historians. The neo-classical method, in itself, led to no dynamic theory.

The Marxist Method

The Marxist economist also follows the broad outline of the Aristotelian method and, like the neo-classicist, concentrates on the second or deductive stage of analysis. However, the Marxist makes a more conscientious effort to correlate his theory with facts, especially the facts of economic and social history. While a certain amount of attention is devoted to individual behaviour, the fundamental unit of Marxist analysis is the group or class. The laws derived from Marxist analysis are mainly aggregative or macro-economic. The analysis is concerned with the laws of equilibrium and motion of the capitalist economy as a whole, rather than with laws pertinent to individual households and firms.

The Marxist argues that there can be no independent *economic* science. Professional economists, like everyone else in society, express the views of their class. Since most professional economists in capitalist societies are employed by academic institutions or governments, both of which are

mere creatures of the ruling capitalist class, most economists
are necessarily apologists for the capitalist system. There is
no such thing as a universal and objective economics, but
only "fascist economics"; "bourgeois economics"; and
"socialist economics". The Marxist is in danger of falling
into his own trap here: for if views on economics are necessarily a reflection of class status, this must be true of Marxist
economics as well. As Professor Knight aptly phrases it:[5]

If discussion itself is mechanically or culturally determined,
or if it can be adequately accounted for (causally), in terms
of individual interests alone, whether these are thought of as
being essentially economic or of whatever kind, then discussion
simply ceases to be discussion. The completely candid Marxist
would have to begin every statement with the observation that
the noise he is about to make is to be regarded as the effect
of appropriate causes, or (really also, at the same time) that
the proposition he is about to utter is purely an expression of
certain (economic) interests of his own ego.

The Marxist would argue, however, that this problem can
be solved by taking into account the effect of the class
structure on economic opinions. An objective *economic*
science is impossible, but an objective *social* science is not.
Thus Marxist theory consists of economics, sociology, politics,
and history intertwined, with technical progress as the main
exogenous variable, affecting the whole social, political and
economic position through the medium of the class struggle.

The great contribution of Marx to economics was the construction of a theory of economic development by the
application of this method. The significance of this contribution has sometimes escaped professional economists of
other schools. When Knight writes that "Marxism is not
merely a romantic simplification, it is intellectually self-
contradictory, and ethically nihilistic and monstrous",[6] he is
confusing three separate aspects of Marxism: the political
and historical conclusions; the inadequacy of the labour
theory of value, which Marx took over with too little

5 F. H. Knight, "Ethics and Economic Reform", *Economica*, August 1939,
pp. 314, 315.
6 *Ibid.*

question from the Classical School; and the Marxist *method*. The *method* consists mainly of treating social development as a unit, or "Gestalt", with economic, sociological and political history treated as parts of a single and inseparable pattern. The "economic interpretation of history" is not a *method*, but a *conclusion* (right or wrong), derived by Marxists from their analytico-historical analysis. Similarly, the treatment of the class war as the medium of social change is not the fundamental Marxist method, but a conclusion. The method consists in treating *whole groups* as conforming to certain patterns of behaviour, as distinct from the "psychological individualism" of the neo-classicists.

The institutionalists, who are completely disassociated from the Marxists politically, share the Marxist opinion regarding method. Indeed, the Marxist approach to theories of economic and social change has the approval of many economists who would never allow themselves to be called either Marxists or Institutionalists, let alone Communists. For example, Adolf Lowe writes of Marx: "His great systematic achievement was the discovery that large scale organization and permanent technical progress determined the structure and dynamics of the capitalist market process."[7] Indeed, it is probably safe to say that *no* consistent theory of capitalist development has yet been produced that is not closely similar to the Marxist theory — whatever the political position of the writer. Joseph Schumpeter, who before his death declared himself in favour of the Corporative State as a means of checking the spread of socialism, is best known in academic circles for his theory of economic development, which is distinctly Marxist in method. It is also worth noticing that although Schumpeter is anti-socialist in his policy recommendations, his economic theory leads him to the conclusion that capitalism must eventually break down.[8]

---

[7] *Op. cit.*, p. 82.
[8] Cf. his *Capitalism, Socialism, and Democracy* (New York 1942); his chapter on "Capitalism in the Postwar World", in *Postwar Economic Problems* (ed. S. E. Harris, New York 1943); and his articles "L'Avenir du Capitalisme", in *Comment Sauvegarder L'Entreprise Privée*, Montreal 1946.

The Institutionalist Method

The Institutionalists follow the footsteps of Thorstein Veblen.[9] They can be sub-divided into two camps, each of which takes its direction from one part of Veblen's teachings to the almost total exclusion of the other. The first branch (which includes such economists as Gambs, Ayres, Ise, and Innis), is continuing Veblen's efforts to develop a social dynamic theory. The second, led by the late Wesley Mitchell and centering around the National Bureau of Economic Research in New York, takes from Veblen his emphasis on the "opaque fact", and restricts its activity to somewhat unimaginative fact-gathering, to the almost total exclusion of explicit economic or social theory of any kind.

The first branch has little interest in theories of equilibrium of household and firm, and not much more interest in theories of equilibrium of economies as a whole. They seek to develop an "evolutionary economics". Like the Marxists, this branch of the Institutionalists' school considers it impossible to isolate economic development from social, political, and general historical development. On the whole, their efforts to develop theories of social development by use of this "Gestalt" method has been less successful than the Marxist, because they are even less willing than Marxists to make simplifications that would permit systematic analysis.

While the broad outline of the Aristotelian method is still discernible in their work, the structure is very loose. Induction and deduction tend to become entangled in a hopeless mess. Similarly, psychological individualism and theories of group behaviour are blended into a characterless melange. As Gambs puts it, the Institutionalists "have made — or, at least, valiantly tried to make — its doctrines conformable to

---

9 It must also be said that Veblen's influence has not been comparable in extent to the influence of Marx, Marshall, and Keynes, who hold roughly the same position with respect to neo-Marxian, neo-classical, and neo-Keynesian economics as Veblen does to Institutionalism. In his article on Veblen in the *Encyclopaedia of the Social Sciences,* Alvin Johnson says very correctly that "a relatively small number of American economists know Veblen well. He is little known to English economists, and virtually unknown to scholars on the European continent."

those of anthropology, ethnology, psychology, genetics".[10] A good example of the results of this kind of economics — if indeed it is economics at all — is provided by Ayres' book on the *Theory of Economic Progress*. The pages are sprinkled with *obiter dicta* on social psychology, anthropology, psychiatry, biology, and politics, interspersed with startling generalizations which often seemed to have little connection with the preceding observations. The theories also assume, without examination, that micro-economic and macro-economic relations are co-determined and therefore mutually consistent.

The method of the second branch of Institutionalists is almost wholly inductive, comprising statistics and history rather than econometrics. That is, it arranges facts according to their sequence in time, without attempting to measure quantitative functional relationships. By the same token, most of its work to date has fallen into the first stage of the Aristotelian approach rather than the third. They promise to use their masses of data to test theories some day or other; meanwhile, they insist that the deductive or the final empirical stages cannot be attempted scientifically until *all* the facts have been gathered. They combine micro- and macro-economics, but place more emphasis on deglomeration than on aggregation.

This branch of the Institutionalist school fails to separate the dead issues of the nineteenth century *Methodenstreit* from the live issues of today. Once the methodological struggle between the German Historical School and the Austrian theoretical school had shown that the Austrians concentrated too much on theory and the Historians too much on facts, few economists have denied that desirability of combining fact and theory in a single analytical process, with a certain amount of division of labour among individual eco-

---

10 *Op. cit.* p. 10. Gambs isolates four chief characteristics of Institutionalist method: use of hypothetico-deduction; concern for the broad generalization; the use of "something like the Hegelian dialectic"; and a "global" or configurationist approach (*op. cit.* p. 60). With such a vague concept of method, it is not surprising that some of the writing of this group is more opaque than factual!

nomists. The late E. F. M. Durbin voiced the opinion of the great majority of economists when he wrote:[11]

The task of the social scientist is therefore the same in all essential principles as that of the natural scientist — to apply logical processes to the data of observation and to attempt the verification of hypothesis on the assumption of the continuity and the determination by general laws, of all events. How can that be done? Within the existing field of economics the first answer is obvious, to give up writing books without theories and books without evidence. Until we are all concerned to prove the theories we hold by an appeal to the facts . . . we shall proceed but slowly to agreement in the light of knowledge.

Yet in his first report as Wesley Mitchell's successor as Research Director of the National Bureau of Economic Research, Arthur F. Burns attacked "the Keynesian thinking of our time" in a manner that smacks of flogging of dead horses. Keynesian theories, Burns insists, and most others too, are far too simple, ignoring many significant facts, which "show that for a period as complicated and turbulent as the 30's it is not difficult to find particular facts that agreeably support any one of several simple hypotheses".[12] Against this danger, "the only real safeguard . . . is thorough scholarship . . . ", that is, collection of more and more facts. "A great deal of new and difficult research will still be necessary, involving studies of national income, agriculture, transportation, construction, mechanization, trade unionism, migration, wages, prices, interest rates, security markets and banking", extending back at least as far as the Civil War. The "mass of information" accumulated by the Bureau in its twenty-five years of operation is just a beginning, and an explanation of the great depression of the 30's "may develop into a series of monographs instead of a single volume". The time is not yet ripe for full-fledged theories of economic fluctuations. "Not a few of our studies abound in subtle theoretical analysis," Burns states, "but they stress especially those observable phenomena of cyclical behaviour which in

11 E. F. M. Durbin, "Methods of Research—A plan for Co-operation in the Social Sciences", *Economic Journal*, June 1938.
12 Arthur F. Burns, *Economic Research and the Keynesian Thinking of Our Time*, 26th Annual Report of the National Bureau of Economic Research, New York, 1946.

commonplace parlance pass as 'facts'. This feature of our work reflects a cool scientific judgment, viz., if business cycles are to be explained reliably, we should have precise and tested knowledge of what the business cycles of actual life have been like."

The Keynesian theories, Burns insists, do not conform to these criteria. "Since Keynes works with an artificially simplified business cycle, it is not surprising that his explanations collide with the facts of experience." For example, whereas Keynes argues that "the collapse of investment brings prosperity to a close, the fact is that orders for machinery, orders for other durable equipment and contracts for different categories of construction often reach cyclical maxima at widely scattered dates". Consequently, aggregates must be broken down. "The breakdown of aggregates not only helps to define the nature of the business cycle problem: it often gives a clue to the processes that link different business factors together."[13]

A partial reply to these charges has been given by Tjalling C. Koopmans, an econometrician working in both neoclassical and Keynesian traditions, in a review of Burns' and Mitchell's *Measuring Business Cycles*.[14] The Burns-Mitchell approach is empirical, Koopmans points out, in the sense that

The various choices as to what to "look for", what economic phenomena to observe, and what measures to define and compute, are made with a minimum of assistance from theoretical conceptions or hypotheses regarding the nature of the economic processes by which the variables studied are generated.

He compares this approach to the "Kepler stage" of celestial mechanics, in contrast to the later and more theoretical approach of Newton. Koopmans argues, however, that the authors do employ a kind of theory in the selection of their data, and that they would have done better to utilize explicit and refined theories rather than implicit and clumsy ones. In short, "even for the purpose of systematic and large scale observation of such a many-sided phenomenon, theoretical

13 *Op. cit.* pp. 19-24.
14 Tjalling C. Koopmans, "Measurement without Theory," *Econometrica*, Aug. 1947.

preconception about its nature cannot be dispensed with, and the authors do so only to the detriment of the analysis."[15]

Koopmans also argues that conclusions derived from this kind of empirical study provide no guides for economic policy. The Institutionalists would probably agree, adding, however, that "no useful policy recommendations can be made until all the facts have been gathered and sorted". Koopmans concludes finally that the data presented are not really very informative because of the lack of theoretical background:

However, the extraction of more information from the data requires that, in addition to the hypotheses subject to the test, certain basic economic hypotheses are formulated as distributional assumptions, which often are not themselves subject to statistical testing from the same data. Of course, the validity of information so obtained is logically conditional upon the validity of the statistically unverifiable aspects of these basic hypotheses. The greater wealth, definiteness, rigour and relevance to specific questions of such conditional information extractable without hypotheses of the kind indicated, provides the *third argument* against the purely empirical approach.

Here then, is a genuine difference of opinion on method. The "opaque fact" branch of Institutionalists insists on staying in the preliminary inductive stage until *all* relevant information is gathered. Other economists insist that a theoretical framework is needed to select facts, that some useful deductions can be made on the basis of presently known facts, and that recommendations for policy *must* be made, even if our knowledge is incomplete.

The Keynesian Method

The Keynesian method, too, is "Aristotelian" in broad outline. Its distinctive feature so far as the first stage is

---

[15] Koopmans points out that the basis for choosing their seven sets of time series to measure cyclical behaviour is based on no more "subtle" theory than the following, quoted from the Burns-Mitchell study:

These series cover processes that rank high among the activities stressed in theoretical studies of business cycles. Partly for this reason, partly because of the comparatively long stretch of time covered by these records, we regard our small sample as fairly satisfactory for the present purpose.

"The choices made," Koopmans continues, "may have been the best possible ones. But 'good' choices mean relevant choices. What is relevant can only be determined with the help of some notions as to the generation of economic fluctuations, and as to their impact on society."

concerned is the emphasis laid on observation of such aggregative quantities as the national income, the level of employment, private investment, consumer spending and the
like. In the deductive stage, Keynesian method is characterized by bold simplification and generalizations about causal
relationships among those aggregates. The approach is therefore mainly macro-economic. However, neo-Keynesians have
devoted considerable energy to the "problem of aggregation";
that is, to proving the consistency of Keynesian macro-
economics with the micro-economics of the neo-classicists.

Keynes' own theory was not truly dynamic: it was a theory
of equilibrium of the economy as a whole, and of movements
from one equilibrium position to another. It had something
to say about the *path* from one equilibrium position to
another, but it did not analyse the *process* of expansion and
contraction in detail, and its theory of trend was rather
loose. These defects are being remedied by such neo-
Keynesian writers as Hansen, Harrod, Domar, and Kalecki,
who are developing theories of trend with Keynesian tools.

The work of Keynesians in the third stage has been
directed towards translating their deduced aggregative laws
into quantitative terms. A good deal of modern econometrics
is carried out within the Keynesian analytical framework.
The consumption and investment functions, cited as
examples of empirical laws in my opening lecture, were
Keynesian in form.

Conclusions

It would be helpful if the differences in method of the
four schools could be illustrated by pointing to their characteristic ways of dealing with particular economic problems.
Such an illustration can scarcely be provided. The differences
in method reflect mainly varying degrees of interest in the
various fields and stages of economic inquiry, and a consequent division of labour among economists that is actually
very useful. Thus virtually all economists would agree that
the "opaque fact" branch of the Institutionalists are doing a
highly useful job in the essential preliminary stage of gather-
ing data; when tackling problems of monopoly, price con-

trol, location of industry, and the like, all competent economists use neo-classical tools, perhaps with an admixture of
neo-Marxist or neo-Keynesian tools on occasion; when concerned with the problems of unemployment and inflation,
they turn to neo-Keynesian techniques; and when faced with
questions of economic and social development many economists, of widely differing political faiths, resort to neo-
Marxist or neo-Veblenian methods.

The business cycle is one subject that has attracted the
attention of all four groups. Even in this field, however, the
similarities of treatment are more striking than the differences, and such differences as there are result from varying
emphasis on particular aspects of economic fluctuations
rather than from fundamental disagreement on their nature
and causes. All four groups agree that economic fluctuations
are related to the operations of the monetary system, especially the credit mechanism; that discrepancies between
planned saving and planned investment are a central feature;
and that distortions of the price-cost structure, due to rigidities and immobilities, are another. There are no specific
theories that can be properly described as "Keynesian",
"neo-classical", "Institutionalist", or even "Marxist". The
neo-classical writers have stressed the role of the credit
system in permitting discrepancies between market and
equilibrium rates of interest to develop, leading to gaps
between planned savings and planned investment and to
distortions of the price-cost structure. The "Institutionalist"
theories of the cycle are much the same. John R. Commons
berates the nineteenth-century neo-classical economists for
failure to explain fluctuations in the price level, a failure
he attributes to inadequate statistical method; but when he
comes to offer an explanation himself, he falls back on a
neo-classical (Wicksellian) theory which runs in terms of
monetary mismanagement, divergencies of market and equilibrium rates of interest, and consequent discrepancies between
savings and investment.[16] The "opaque fact" or National
Bureau branch emphasize leads and lags in the price-cost
structure, but are reluctant to formulate general theories.

---

16 *Institutional Economics* (New York 1935), especially pp. 124 and 605 ff.

Marxist theory of economic fluctuations is again a matter of divergencies between savings and investment, booms resulting (mainly) from the high profits associated with technological progress and depressions (mainly) from under-consumption; the Marxist chooses language that lays more stress on the role of inequalities of income and the underlying class structure than others, but that is the main difference. The Keynesian theory is also a savings-and-investment theory, with booms explained in terms of a high "marginal efficiency of capital" — which really boils down to high prospective profits on new investment — and depressions explained in terms of under-consumption and excessive liquidity preference (desire to hold cash balances). The "acceleration principle", a tool developed by National-Bureau-Institutionalist J. M. Clark, has been incorporated into the business cycle theories of such neo-Keynesians as Harrod and Samuelson. Any competent economist setting out to write a textbook on business cycles today would certainly incorporate the work of all four schools.

Finally, it is necessary to state again that the pictures I have drawn of these four schools are really caricatures, at least so far as economic analysis is concerned. Few economists would recognize themselves in these drawings. Of the five thousand members of the American Economic Association (for example) I doubt whether a hundred could be classified in terms of this quadrachotomy, in a manner that would be satisfactory both to themselves and to a board of judges comprised, let us say, of the officials of the Association. Even such a neo-Keynesian economist as Paul Samuelson has recently written, "I myself am not a Keynesian, though I have many friends who are." Some of his friends might say the same.[17] To find meaningful differences of opinion among economists, we must leave economics and turn to politics.

---

17 Where would I put myself? My basic training, my early publications, and some recent ones, were distinctly neo-classical; two of my major undertakings have been part of the programme of the National Bureau of Economic Research; my recent writings have had a distinctly Keynesian bent; and some of my essays on economic history and the theory of economic development might conceivably pass as Marxist.

Political Differences

By whom, and for whom, should economic planning be undertaken? This question is the issue of our era. Political differences within the western democracies spring largely from divergent views on the answers to this question. The growing friction in international relations results mainly from the clash of two rival ideologies concerning them. Since economists are also people, there is no reason to expect them to provide identical answers to this question. Differences of opinion among economists regarding the relative importance of freedom and security, and about the kind of political framework that is most conducive to economic efficiency, is no more evidence of disagreement on the fundamental principles of their science than are different attitudes towards socialized medicine among medical doctors. At the same time, there is a certain relationship between the methodological differences noted above and the differences in political viewpoint among the four main groups. It is consequently a matter of some interest, and of no little importance, to trace the relationship.

The School of Latter-day Laissez-faire

The neo-classical economists believe that there should be as little centralized economic planning as possible; that economic planning should be done almost entirely by individual households and firms; and that the role of government should be restricted to laying down the institutional and legal framework and enforcing the law. The "Chamber of Commerce" branch of this school goes somewhat further, contending that the legal framework should be designed to promote "good business", on the grounds that what is good for business is necessarily good for society as a whole. This attitude is well expressed in a recent publication of the United States Chamber of Commerce:

Under our economic system, the government has confined its activities, at least until within the last decade or two, largely to keeping law and order, serving as umpire, enforcing competition, establishing the currency, and carrying on certain major activities such as highways, education, sanitation and a few others which were believed generally to be beyond the competence of individual enterprise. . . . A free economic society is essentially voluntary; directives, orders and regimentation are kept at a minimum. This economic system may be described as a free market economy; the individuals are loosely knit together through voluntary co-operation under which each expresses his participation by his demand for and supplying of goods and services through the free pricing system.[18]

The Keynesians

The Keynesians insist on as much centralized planning as is necessary to maintain full employment without inflation, to improve the allocation of resources, to reduce the inequality of the distribution of income, and to stimulate economic progress. Most Keynesians would probably argue that policies for the achievement of these objectives must be formulated originally by experts, many of whom would necessarily be in the government employ; but they would also demand that the legislation and execution of the plans be carried out through the usual machinery of responsible and democratic government. Finally, the planning would be done — as the list of objectives itself suggests — for society at large.

For the most part, Keynesians do not much care whether the good life is attained under capitalism or under socialism. They feel that they can formulate effective economic policies for either system, and that either system can be made to work well. At the same time, they recognize that both systems present extraordinary political and administrative difficulties in executing the policies. Different Keynesians assess differently the relative possibilities of achieving economic goals and basic freedoms in the two systems; accordingly, despite agreement on economic grounds, some Keynesians fall on one side of the political fence, some on the other, while a good many remain perched precariously on the fence itself.

The Marxists

Paradox though it may seem, the Marxists are the one group of economists who aim ultimately at the complete absence of economic planning by the state. Under full-

18 *The American Competitive Enterprise System,* Chamber of Commerce of the United States, 1946, pp. 5 and 6.

fledged Communism, society would be classless and therefore stateless; for, according to Marxist theory, the state is simply one of the instruments by which the dominant economic class carries out its aims. Under Communism, "government over people" gives way to "administration of things". Moreover, once full-fledged Communism is achieved, universal abundance will prevail, all members of society will share in the national income according to their needs, and no conflict will arise in the satisfaction of individual wants. Consequently, a system of anarchy will serve society in a perfectly smooth and orderly fashion. However, in the transitional stage of "socialism", which most Marxists expect to last a very long time,[19] economic planning must be extended to every aspect of production and distribution of goods and services. Planning will be done by the "proletariat", through their chosen representatives; and the planning will be done for the workers, defined so as to include all "useful" members of society.

The Institutionalists

The Institutionalists are even harder to classify politically than the other three groups. The "National Bureau" branch of the school is characterized mainly by its refusal to take sides politically.[20] However, they seem to dislike monopolies,

---

[19] Anarchist ideas play a very small role in modern Marxism. Cf. Lenin, *State and Revolution*, London 1933, pp. 15-20.

[20] True, I once heard a prominent member of this group, in the privacy of his home and under the influence of alcohol, confess that in his opinion there was little to choose between Democrats and Republicans, the superiority of the former in federal politics being offset by their inferiority in local politics!

A typical statement is made by John R. Commons in his major work, *Institutional Economics* (pp. 611-612):

"We close the writing of this book in November 1933. For the past eight months — the first time in history — a great nation has directed its leader to show them the way to a managed recovery instead of the automatic recoveries after all preceding depressions. Only twice before, at the conclusion of two great war cycles, 1847 and 1897, have similar depths been reached. But this time, in less than 13 years, instead of 30 or more years, after the war peak of decisive prosperity, have nations taken it into their hands to bring about a managed recovery instead of leaving it to natural law. Beginning with the Communism of Lenin, the Fascism of Mussolini, and extending to the Democracy of Roosevelt, the Nazism of Hitler, the Militarism of Japan, different nations, in their own way, have sought a managed recovery from the wars of their capitalistic civilizations. . . .

"In the midst of the kaleidoscopic changes every day no *book* or succession

and occasionally their opposition to Keynesian method spills over into mild opposition to Keynesian policies. On the rare occasions on which they commit themselves to policy statements, Mitchell and Burns end up not far from the "latter-day laissez-faire" group. Clark, however, is willing to sanction a modicum of Keynesian policy.

The "evolutionary economics" branch is somewhat to the left of the "opaque fact" branch politically, clustering somewhere near the Keynesian position. They are social reformers for the most part, favouring a "managed economy", with government intervention where necessary. In the United States, many of them found shelter beneath the wings of the "Blue Eagle". Indeed, the first Roosevelt administration owed a good deal to the intellectual leadership of such institutionalist economists as Tugwell, Warren, and Mayer. The second "New Deal" Administration was a good deal more Keynesian in tone, but the "evolutionists" did not find themselves too uncomfortable under it.[21]

The Assessment of Capitalism

These divergent attitudes towards economic planning rest mainly upon differences in assessment of the vices and virtues of capitalism, which in turn result largely from the methodological differences already noted.

The Laissez-Faire School

The neo-classicists, because of their concentration on micro-economics, tend to think of the free private enterprise

---

of books can come out rapidly enough to keep up with the turnover of civilizations. The matter is one for daily, hourly, weekly publications. A book can only develop general principles and methods of investigation. The author and all others must turn, guided as they choose to be by principles and methods, to the immediate urgent problems which crowd upon all of them more or less alike. No one can foretell what either a great leader will do or what nations will do. We leave them at this point, and we watch and participate, each in his own little corner as opportunity may offer, from day to day, and week to week."

21 It is not unlikely that Veblen was the author of the term "new deal" in the sense of social reform. In discussing the Marxist theory of capitalist breakdown, he wrote: "It may be that the working classes will go forward along the line of the socialistic ideals and enforce a new deal, in which there shall be no economic class discrepancies, no international animosity, no dynastic politics" (He added that the workers might, on the other hand, "sink their force in the broad sands of patriotism"). "The Socialist Economics of Karl Marx", in *The Place of Science in Modern Civilisation*, New York 1919, p. 442.

system as *intrinsically* competitive, flexible, and efficient. It is prevented from functioning perfectly at all times only by lags, frictions, price rigidities (particularly rigidities in wage rates and interest rates), and by misguided government intervention in economic affairs. An essential aspect of the Chamber of Commerce variant of this theory is that *both* savings and investment must be encouraged if economic progress is to continue.[22] Finally, having no theory of economic or social development, the neo-classical school tends to regard capitalism as something that was in the beginning and ever shall be; they are usually acquainted with economic history, but they fail to draw its moral.

The latter-day *laissez-faire* economist accordingly believes that the capitalist system can be preserved merely by removing its institutional imperfections. He supports the anti-trust laws, often with the rider that similar legislation is necessary to check the growing power of "Labour monopolies". He recommends the reduction or abolition of taxes which are either unjustly regressive, or discouraging to savings and investment. He favours legislation to control the operation of the banking system, so as to alleviate the variations of credit supply which he links closely with economic fluctuations as a whole. He still hopes to find "the" cause of the business cycle. Having found it, he would then perform a simple operation to remove the cancer, after which the economic organism would remain healthy without further treatment by government doctors. Meanwhile, he prefers measures for "built-in flexibility" of government expenditures and revenues (such as unemployment insurance and progressive tax structures) to measures requiring administrative discretion (such as countercyclical variation of public investment outlays and tax rates). Needless to say, the *laissez-faire* economist is usually violently anti-socialist.

---

[22] Cf. Swanson and Schmidt, *Economic Stagnation or Progress,* Washington (U.S. Chamber of Commerce, 1946), pp. 170-172; Committee on Public Debt Policy, *Our National Debt and Our Savings,* New York 1947, pp. 4-7; and B. Higgins, "To Save or Not to Save," *Canadian Journal of Economics and Political Science,* February 1948, and "Savings and Welfare in the World Economy," *Economia Internationale,* November 1950.

Keynesian Political Economy

Keynesian economic theory, with its macro-economic approach, leads to the conclusion that full employment equilibrium is a "special case", unlikely to appear often in a capitalist society in which management of economic affairs is left to businessmen, investors and consumers alone. The theory also suggests the strong possibility that in highly developed economies there will be a *chronic* tendency for savings to exceed investment at high levels of employment, leading to continuous and growing unemployment, unless appropriate policies are adopted. The Keynesian theory, therefore, resembles the Marxist theory in suggesting a tendency for capitalist economies to perform less and less satisfactorily as they mature. However, it is also a major conclusion of Keynesian political economy that bad performance of capitalist economies is *unnecessary*, and that expert management by government *can* make the capitalist system function efficiently.

The Keynesian recommends mainly policies for the guarantee of an adequate flow of total spending — enough to maintain full employment but not so much as to create inflation. He selects these policies in such a way as to promote simultaneously the improvement of income distribution, a more efficient allocation of resources, and healthy economic expansion. Contrary to the neo-classicist, he does not believe that these objectives can be obtained by surgery alone; on the contrary, he believes that the sick capitalist economy will need more or less continuous treatment if it is to give a semblance of health in its day-to-day working. He considers fluctuations in private spending to be inherent in a private enterprise economy, and points out that no workable *automatic* system can be designed to offset these fluctuations. Consequently, he recommends government expenditures for social welfare and economic development, varying inversely with the volume of private spending over the business cycle; he would reduce taxes (especially taxes on lower income groups) in periods of depression, and raise them (especially on higher income groups) when inflation

threatens. The expenditures recommended include such projects as slum clearance, low rental housing, and urban re-
development; soil conservation, flood control, and river valley
development; family allowances, old-age pensions, and unemployment insurance; government sharing of risks of
private investment; government gifts and loans to expand
foreign trade; and so forth.

Finally, Keynesians have considerable faith in the power
of ideas, and believe that the general public can be persuaded
to support, and even to demand, the kind of policies which
Keynesians consider effective. This view has been well
expressed by Keynes himself:[23]

But apart from this contemporary mood, the ideas of economists and political philosophers, both when they are right and
when they are wrong, are more powerful than is commonly
understood. Indeed the world is ruled by little else. Practical
men, who believe themselves to be quite exempt from any
intellectual influences, are usually the slaves of some defunct
economist. Madmen in authority, who hear voices in the air, are
distilling their frenzy from some academic scribbler of a few
years back. I am sure that the power of vested interests is vastly
exaggerated compared with the gradual encroachment of ideas.
Not, indeed, immediately, but after a certain interval; for in the
field of economic and political philosophy there are not many
who are influenced by new theories after they are twenty-five
or thirty years of age, so that the ideas which civil servants and
politicians and even agitators apply to current events are not
likely to be the newest. But, soon or late, it is ideas, not vested
interests which are dangerous for good or evil.

The Marxist View

As already noted, Marxist economic theory is primarily a
theory of capitalist development. The general theory — including its sociological and political as well as its economic
aspects — leads to the conclusion that capitalism must
ultimately break down. The key phenomenon of the Marxist
theory is the tendency for the rate of profit to decline as a
country advances to a high degree of capitalistic development; falling profits lead inevitably to imperialist wars, and
to the squeezing of labour, in an effort to prevent a further

---

23 J. M. Keynes, *The General Theory of Employment, Interest, and Money,*
pp. 383-384.

fall; and this ruthless exploitation by the ruling class leads ultimately to the collapse of capitalism, through the revolt of the working class.

This theory provides no basis for policy recommendations within the capitalist framework. Marxists will, of course, have views about particular economic policies proposed for capitalist countries, but these views will not be based upon Marxist economic analysis of the effectiveness of these policies for achieving the objectives for which the capitalist government proposes them. The Marxist will consider them rather from the point of view of their immediate impact upon the condition of the workers and from the ultimate effect upon the advent of capitalist collapse. Here the Marxist has sometimes found himself in a dilemma, for a policy which would improve the lot of the worker in the short-run might postpone the complete collapse of capitalism and the establishment of the socialist state. Anglo-American Marxists, when faced with this dilemma, have usually backed social reforms which seemed to them to bring clear-cut short-run gains to the working class.

Moreover, Marxist economic theory does not provide a basis for *socialist* economic planning either, as Lenin himself once pointed out.[24] Apart from a few references to the transition from socialism to communism and the "withering away of the state", Marxist theory provides no guide for the day-to-day decisions that must be made by administrators of a socialist economy. In the U.S.S.R., policies closely akin to those of the Keynesian and neo-classical economists have finally been evolved by trial and error, with a degree of bungling and hardship which could have been avoided if these principles had been understood from the beginning. Even now, the refusal to relinquish an inadequate labour theory of value for a more complete theory taking account of relative intensity of desire ("elasticity of substitution" in neo-classical terminology), as well as all relevant social costs, results in some inefficiency and misallocation of resources.[25]

[24] Cf. E. H. Carr, *The Soviet Impact on the Western World,* New York 1947, p. 23.
[25] See, for example, the citations from the Soviet Press in Harry Schwartz, *Russia's Postwar Economy,* Syracuse, 1947, pp. 36-40.

Marxists have been somewhat perturbed by the development of Keynesian economic analysis and policies. The Keynesian agrees with the Marxist that the capitalist system works badly, and that it will tend to work worse as time goes by; but the Keynesian also suggests policies designed to make capitalism — or at least a "mixed" system — work perfectly well. Now if capitalism can be made to work well, why must it break down? In their answer to this question, Marxists fall into two groups. The attitude of the first group is that the Keynesian economic analysis is essentially valid, and that their policy recommendations might work if adopted, but that they have no chance of being adopted in the capitalist system. Thus Paul M. Sweezy writes:[26]

When we turn to the question of the relation between economics and politics, we shall find that the Keynesians hold a *deus ex machina* theory of the state. They are not all agreed on what the state should do, but each has his own recipe for full employment, higher living standards, and lasting prosperity. These programmes for the most part are logically consistent and highly persuasive. They make the task of social betterment sound easy, or if not easy at any rate uncomplicated. What is needed is education (naturally along Keynesian lines), for when people —at least the right people—come to understand what is the matter and how it can be remedied, can there be any doubt about the outcome? What the Keynesians overlook, or at least completely miss the implications of, is that every one of these schemes which deserves to be taken seriously would involve redistributing income in favour of the poor, curtailing the power of capital, and enhancing the power of labour. It is simply utopian to expect the state in a society where all the levers of control are in the hands of the capitalist class to embark upon such a course.

Similarly, Lawrence Klein argues:[27]

Keynes, it has been stressed, is not a radical. He wanted to reform capitalism in order to make it work better and to preserve it. How is it possible that any capitalist could object to a policy of the preservation of capitalism? The answer is that many capitalists are unaware of the precarious state of the system during a period of serious depression, and do not see the proper relationship between their own position and that of the system

---

26 Paul M. Sweezy, "Marxian and Orthodox Economics," *Science and Society*, Summer, 1947, p. 233.
27 Lawrence R. Klein, *The Keynesian Revolution*, New York, 1947, p. 194.

as a whole. It is inevitable that most of the effective measures listed in the full-employment legislation above will be strongly opposed by some group of the capitalist population.

The second group of Marxists goes farther in their criticism, insisting that the Keynesian analysis involves critical errors and that, consequently, the Keynesian policies could not make capitalism work really well even if they were adopted. Mr. Foster, for example, insists[28] that

Keynesism cannot achieve its avowed goal of permanent full employment within the framework of the capitalist system. This is so because it does not remove the fundamental cause of mass unemployment, namely, the basic contradiction between the social character of production and the private character of appropriation. Keynesism deals with symptoms, not basic causes. Lenin says: "Gigantic crashes have become possible and inevitable, only because powerful social productive forces have become subordinated to a gang of rich men, whose only concern is to make profits." The molehill of government public works expenditures cannot offset the mountain of surplus value stolen from the workers by the capitalists.

The Institutionalist View

The "National Bureau" group is non-committal about the efficiency and survival of capitalism, as about everything else. On the whole, however, they seem to feel that if institutional frictions, lags, monopoly restrictions, and so forth, could be removed, capitalist economies would operate with reasonable efficiency.

Considering the obviously close relationship between the method of Marx and of the "evolutionary" institutionalists, it is remarkable that the latter group have not been further to the left than they have been. Veblen himself was regarded as something of a radical in his day. Veblen's writings were largely in reaction against the doctrines of his teacher, J. B. Clark, and of the economist-theologians who filled most of the chairs in American universities in Veblen's day. So much of the literature to which Veblen was subjected as a student was really second-rate moral philosophy, designed to justify an obviously imperfect economic order, that one can hardly

---

28 William Z. Foster, "The Political Significance of Keynesism," *Political Affairs*, January 1948.

blame Veblen for rebelling.[29] Yet his rebellion, and that of
his followers, did not crystallize into support of a particular
form of economic and social order, as Marx's did. Perhaps
Veblen's "shotgun" method explains the rather discursive
nature of his views on social reform.

Veblen himself was rather critical of socialist theory,
especially its Marxist branch. It is not true, he insisted,[30]

that the institution(s) of private property under free competition . . . have worked to the detriment of the material
interests of the average member of society. . . . Especially can it
fairly be claimed that the result of the last few decades of our
industrial development has been to increase greatly the creature
comforts within the reach of the average human being. And
decidedly the result has been an amelioration of the lot of the
less favoured in a relatively greater degree than that of those
economically more fortunate.

The trouble is rather that in capitalist societies — especially
in America — social status and prestige depends on a man's
relative position on the income scale. Class friction there
certainly is, but it is not "material" but "economic". Whether
socialization will improve matters is questionable:[31]

Certainly, the fact that constitutional government — the
nationalization of political functions — seems to have been a
move in the right direction is not to be taken as proof of the
advisability of forthwith nationalizing the industrial functions.
At the same time this fact does afford ground for the claim that
a movement in this direction may prove itself in some degree
advantageous, even if it takes place at a stage in the development of human nature at which mankind is still far from being
entirely fit for the duties which the new system shall impose.
The question, therefore, is not whether we have reached the
perfection of character which would be necessary in order to a
perfect working of the scheme of nationalization of industry, but
whether we have reached such a degree of development as would
make an imperfect working of the scheme possible.

Veblen had much admiration for Marx, but nevertheless
considered his system a mixture of bad Darwinism, bad
Hegelianism, and bad economic theory. The "unteleological

---

29 See Joseph Dorfman, *Thorstein Veblen and His America* (New York
1934), especially Chapters IV and VI-IX. For a brief account of Veblen's life
and works, see J. A. Hobson, *Veblen*, London, 1936.
30 *The Place of Science in Modern Civilization*, p. 391.
31 *Ibid.* pp. 407-8.

Darwinian concept of natural selection" would never have led to "the Marxian notion of a conscious class struggle", let alone to "the classless economic structure of the socialist final term. In Darwinism there is no such final or perfect term, and no definitive equilibrium."[32]

But Marxism "is also not legitimately Hegelian, whether of the Right or the Left. It is of a utilitarian origin and of English pedigree. . . . It is in fact a piece of hedonism, and is related to Bentham rather than Hegel."[33] As for the labour theory value, Marx "offers inadequate proof"; indeed, "he offers no proof of it".[34] Veblen summarizes his assessment of Marx in highly derogatory terms:[35]

Nothing much need be said as to the tenability of this theory. In its essentials, or at least in its characteristic elements, it has for the most part been given up by latter-day socialist writers. The number of those who hold to it without essential deviation is growing gradually smaller. Such is necessarily the case, and for more than one reason. The facts are not bearing it out on certain critical points, such as the doctrine of increasing misery; and the Hegelian philosophical postulates, without which the Marxism of Marx is groundless, are for the most part forgotten by the dogmatists of today. Darwinism has largely supplanted Hegelianism in their habits of thought.

The political position of present day "evolutionary institutionalists" is still less clearly defined than Veblen's. In his "reappraisal of institutional economics", Gambs suggests that Veblen's work reveals other politico-economic questions to ask than "Are you for or against the Soviet Union?" (p. 2). Neo-Veblenians, he says, have been more prone than neoclassicists to espouse schemes for reform because "they have never felt . . . that the clumsy hand of human intervention could disturb the finer workers of the invisible hand" (p. 17). Contemporary institutionalists preserve Veblen's "strong utopian bias" (p. 22). But what this Utopia is to be, we are not told.

Finally, the Institutionalists array themselves on the side of Marx, and against the Keynesians, in arguing that government policy tends to reflect the economic interests of powerful groups, and that economic ideas follow policies rather

---

[32] *Ibid.* pp. 416-417.　　[33] *Ibid.* pp. 417-418.　　[34] *Ibid.* p. 419.　　[35] *Ibid.* p. 429.

than the other way round. Gambs quotes with approval an article of Otto v. Mehring — suggesting even that it could have been written by the Master himself — containing the following passage:[36]

Pareto's opinion is directly opposed to the Keynesian and it seems worth while to dwell upon this important topic somewhat longer. The famous Italian author distinguishes between (A) the psychic state of a people, that is, in great part the product of individual interests, economic, political and social, and of the circumstances under which people live, (B) the conduct, namely, the actual management of affairs, and (C) the theory... Pareto insists that there is a strong relation A → B and A → C, but generally only a tenuous relation C → B. . . .

If one applies Pareto's reasoning to the general ideas of the classical school as well as to Mr. Keynes' theory, the argument would run approximately as follows: The interests and sentiments of the rising class of the eighteenth century, which became the ruling class of the nineteenth century, i.e., the bourgeoisie (A), determined the practical policy of nonintervention by the government (B), and the theory of individualistic economy (C). On the other hand, the interests of the working class, whose power was greatly increased during the latter part of the nineteenth and during the twentieth century (A), are bringing about the policy of social ("progressive") liberalism (B), and create the Keynesian theory (C), with its concepts of liquidity preference, entrepreneurs' psychological expectations and propensity to consume.

Thus the Institutionalist raises the same question regarding Keynesian policies for full employment without inflation as the Marxist: Are these policies in conformity with the Gestalt of the western democracies? Gambs thinks that Veblen would have answered "No" — at least for America (p. 26). And here, Gambs argues, one can see the great usefulness of the Gestalt concept: it is an excellent desire "for screening out economic plans or innovations that are incongruous with the Gestalt". If any policy proposal violates the Gestalt, "we might as well abandon the plan".

Conclusions

We began this lecture by saying that economists agree

---

[36] Otto von Mering, "Some Problems of Methodology in Modern Economic Theory," *American Economic Review*, xxxiv, pp. 87-98.

on a good deal . . . enough to formulate answers, satisfactory to the majority of professional economists, to any policy question that is clearly put. We went on to say that economists do disagree on certain matters on the frontiers of knowledge, as all scientists do, but that such disagreement is a symptom of scientific progress. We then pointed out that a methodological distinction could be made among four "schools" of economists, but the distinction turned out to rest largely on differing interests within the field of economics and a necessary division of labour. Finally, we saw that a somewhat artificial division could be made into the same four groups in terms of political faith and attitude towards capitalism; but political differences do not betray lack of agreement on scientific principles, and individual economists falling in one methodological school often fall in another political group. In sum, economists disagree on three things: Are certain recently formulated propositions true? How can new laws, especially dynamic laws, best be discovered? What is the best political system? None of these controversies prevents competent economists from reaching agreement on specific policy problems.

Two generations ago, the great Italian economist Enrico Barone said that in the final analysis, there are only two schools of economists, "good" and "bad". It is more important today than ever before that the general public should learn to distinguish between *these* two schools. How can it be done? A good economist, like a good carpenter, is recognized not by the manners of his friends, by his tastes, or even by his political views, but by the extent of his acquaintance with the tools of his trade, and the competence and responsibility with which he uses them. Above all, the good economist is characterized by his interest in discovering and promulgating the truth for its own sake, whatever the social or political implications of this truth.

"Good" economists in this sense are to be found in all four camps. There are, perhaps, more to be found among the Keynesians than anywhere else. The Keynesians are on the whole less eager than other economists to sell a particular brand of social system; they are less inclined than others to reason from preconceived convictions regarding the relative merits of socialism and of free private enterprise; they are better able to regard both systems as administrative devices, rather than ends in themselves. They are consequently in a better position to examine both with a dispassionate eye. But these statements apply much more clearly to a comparison of good economists with others than they do to a comparison of Keynesians with others, especially since good economists are usually hard to classify in any other terms.

III

THE OBJECTIVES OF ECONOMIC POLICY AND HOW TO ATTAIN THEM

IN MY FIRST LECTURE I argued that economists know enough to bring about a substantial improvement in standards of living, if given the legal powers needed to institute and administer appropriate policies. In my second lecture I pointed out that economists disagree on certain problems at the frontiers of knowledge, on certain details of methodology, and on politics. The first kind of disagreement, I contended, is a symptom of healthy progress in any field of knowledge. The second resolves itself into differences in taste and interest within the field of economics and a useful division of economists' labour among various problems. The last kind of disagreement, I suggested, is to be expected in a world where political views vary so widely; and diverging opinions on methodology and politics would not prevent a team of "good" economists from reaching agreement on matters of policy, provided the objectives of economic policy were clearly stated. Our next step, obviously, must be to discuss the objectives of economic policy, and to say something about the kind of measures needed to attain them.

Value Judgments and the Approach to Policy

There are two alternative approaches for the economist with respect to economic policy. The first is to accept the objectives laid down by his government. In the United States, the United Kingdom, Canada, Australia and in other countries, governments have declared their intention to maintain full employment without inflation, to provide greater economic security, to improve the income distribution, to accelerate the rate of economic expansion, and to improve the allocation of resources. This list of objectives is quite acceptable to most economists.

However, as stated by governments, these objectives are seldom clearly defined. The economist, who is working with economic concepts and knows the true nature of "economic efficiency" better than someone unacquainted with economic concepts, should be able to define the objectives of economic policy more accurately than could a legislature or even a cabinet minister. Also, the economist can warn the government and the electorate of unknown or forgotten dangers in particular kinds of economic situations. Some countries, for example, have yet to experience hyper-inflation. The economist can warn the public of what hyper-inflation involves, from his knowledge of the experience of other countries, such as the central European countries where hyper-inflation took place after World War I, and his knowledge of the process of hyper-inflation. Similarly, the economist can remind the public of the dangers linked with depression. It is so long now since we have had serious unemployment that a good many people appear to have forgotten the suffering and the threats to social stability it entails. For these reasons, the economist usually feels compelled to formulate economic objectives himself. When economists make public pronouncements on policy, they always have some objectives in mind, although too often the objectives are not explicitly stated.

If we were to set out to draw up a list of objectives which would allow objective and scientific analysis of policy proposals, what criteria would the objectives themselves have to meet? First, the objectives must be non-controversial, in the sense that any intelligent man of goodwill must accept them as desirable *in themselves*. Secondly, they must be unambiguous. If possible, they should be capable of reduction to measurable or quantitative terms; at least, they should be cast in terms that make it possible to recognize to what extent the objectives have been achieved. Finally, the stated objectives must not conflict with any unstated ends. When people say that they are not in favour of full employment, they do not mean that they think full employment is in itself a bad thing; they mean that they do not want full employment if it is to be obtained through a degree of government intervention and control which they dislike, or because they think they can make higher profits by having enough unemployment to undermine the bargaining power of the wage-earners, or that the guarantee of full employment destroys

self-reliance, or something of the sort. The trouble here is
that there are unstated objectives which conflict with the
stated ones. If we are to have a thoroughly objective analysis
of the routes to economic goals, we must state *all* the goals
of economic policy.

In drawing up such a list of economic goals, the economist
usually makes two fundamental value judgments; that is,
statements about things he *believes,* as distinct from things
he *knows.* First, the economist believes that economic policy
should be designed to give people what they want; that is, he
believes that it is "good" for people to be happy. Second, he
believes that, other things being equal, people are made
happier by having more goods and services and leisure to
consume. He does not *know* either of these things. One could
imagine a theological cult arguing that it is a very bad thing
for people to be happy on earth, on the grounds that
temporal happiness might result in a reduction of eternal
happiness. Similarly, one might construct a moral philosophy
which would say that goods and services and leisure are very
bad things. However, the economist's value judgments stand
up very well under philosophical scrutiny.

Is a set of objectives based on value judgments necessarily
unscientific? I think not. All practitioners in any technical
field make value judgments whenever they make recommendations. Consider the medical doctor. He *believes* that
physical health is a "good" thing; or, if he does not believe
that, he at least believes that it is a "good" thing for himself
to be rich, which is also a value judgment. In either case, he
believes, when he treats a patient and tries to cure him, that
he is doing a "good" thing. Similarly, the engineer thinks he
does a good thing if his buildings stand upright, and the
architect thinks it is a good thing for roofs not to leak.

It is important that value judgments should be explicitly
stated, and that they should not be mixed up with scientific
analysis. For example, if an economist allows a belief that
usury is sinful to colour his analysis of how interest rates are
in fact determined, he is a bad economist; he uses bad
method. Or, if he believes that socialism in any form is a
bad thing and allows that belief to influence his analysis

of the effectiveness of public works policy as a means of maintaining full employment, he is a bad economist. But he is not a bad economist if he says: "I believe that socialism is a bad thing" and then proceeds to analyse the operations of the socialist system in a purely objective manner from there on. Value judgments are certainly not on the same footing as scientific principles. As O. H. Taylor puts it:[1]

In the political climate of today in the western democratic world, economists and laymen alike are more than ever involved in the old perpetual debate over economic freedom versus governmental and group controls. . . . There is an evergrowing mass of relevant knowledge, both in economics and other sciences; but even in its fullest sum this knowledge can never become decisive for the question. The reason is that all opinions on the matter necessarily involve, in addition to whatever knowledge they may partly rest on, inherently unprovable value judgments, which are often mere prejudices but, at best, are reflective, philosophical convictions.

It is possible, however, to know something about values. Value judgments should be able to withstand objective philosophical scrutiny. For example, one can be quite sure that suffering is (*ceteris paribus*) bad. We also know that unemployment brings suffering. F. H. Knight writes:[2]

The scientific mind can rest only in one of two extreme positions, that there are absolute values, or that every individual desire is an absolute and one as "good" as another. But neither of these is true; we must learn to think in terms of "value-standards" which have validity of a more subtle kind. It is the higher goal of conduct to test and try these values, to define and improve them, rather than to accept and "satisfy" them. There are no rules for judging values, and it is the worst of errors to attempt to make rules — beyond the rule to "use good judgment"; but it is also most false to assert that one opinion is as good as another, that *de gustibus non est disputandum*.

Similarly, Wilhelm Röpke argues:[3]

The question which for more than a generation has been occupying us in all those sciences to which judgments of such sort are peculiar extends to whether the dignity and the authority of Science can be claimed for these matters which are not merely

---

[1] O. H. Taylor, "The Economics of a 'Free' Society: Four Essays", *The Quarterly Journal of Economics*, November 1948, p. 5.
[2] F. H. Knight, *The Ethics of Competition, op. cit.*, pp. 39-40.
[3] Wilhelm Röpke, *Civatas Humana*, London, 1948, pp. 73-74.

simple demonstrations of "facts" but pass on into positive recommendations or rejection, in short, for so-called value judgments in contra-distinction to statements of fact. There can be no doubt, however, that he who unreservedly would deny scientific legitimacy to judgments of value narrows the sphere of science in a scientifically non-tenable way, and is at the same time adopting a standpoint which can only be disastrous for society as a whole, since this would be to rob society of a genuine leadership in things of the mind, a leadership more necessary than ever at the present time. . . . It is undeniable that there is a peculiarity about value judgments which renders these different from other judgments. If we group all possible judgments together, the first group will be that rigorously logical and cogent one of the type that "A cannot at the same time be not A". In the next group come the empirical judgments, the truth of which can be established through experiment when all due allowance has been made for faulty observation. The third and last group comprises judgments of value. Now it is indisputable that these three groups possess a thoroughly different logical structure and that the logical character of the last group is the weakest. Moreover, it is obvious that it is this last group which passes into the sphere of unscientific statements. About all this there is general agreement. But the question remains, where is the line to be drawn? Whether between the second and third groups as the Relativists (Positivists) demand, or within the third group. The last is the proper answer which settles the difficulty. This demarcation effectively bans all political whimsicalities, arguments and ideologies from the sphere of Science, without shutting its mouth when it is a question of ultimate and highest values and without robbing Science of the possibility of taking up a critical attitude towards pseudo-scientific values.

The Objectives of Economic Policy

With this foundation, we can proceed to lay down the concrete objectives of economic policy. The overall objective, of course, is an optimum allocation of resources; that is, an allocation of every unit of land, labour, capital and management that will contribute as much to human happiness as is possible through production and distribution of goods and services, including leisure.

This objective requires, first of all, cooking as big a "pie" as possible — maximizing real national income (including leisure). In order to maximize the total pie to be sliced up among members of society, all available resources must be utilized, and they must be utilized in the way which will contribute most to satisfaction. That is, maximizing national income requires full employment and an optimal distribution of resources among various goods and services, including leisure. The "right" amount of resources must be devoted to producing beer and the right amount to producing Bibles, in the sense that the last unit of resources applied to the production of beer brings as much satisfaction as the same unit of resources devoted to the production of Bibles.

In addition, policy should be designed to make the pie *grow* at an optimal rate; that is, there must be an optimal rate of economic expansion. This objective requires that technological progress should proceed as quickly as possible —at the maximum rate; it also requires an optimal rate of capital accumulation, the optimum ratio of savings and investments to national income. Apart from technological progress, the "pie" is made to grow by saving out of current income, and investing the savings in new plant, equipment, housing, and inventories, so that the stream of goods and services can be greater in the future. Obviously, it is possible for the proportion of resources directed to building up productive equipment to be too low. It seems to be too low in China, where net capital accumulation proceeds too slowly to bring significant rises in per capita income. It is also possible for the rate of capital accumulation to be too high, in the sense that current sacrifices of consumption are unjustifiably onerous. Such seems to have been the case in Russia during the first and second five-year plans. It was good for us later that the Ukrainian peasant lived on subsistence level (or lower) in order that Russian industrial capacity could be built up; without it, we would almost certainly have lost the war against Germany. But, from a purely economic point of view, it is pushing things a bit too far to build new dams, railways, roads, power plants, and factories at such a rate that some people starve in the process. It is never *economically* justified to devote so many resources to building up capital equipment, and so little to providing for current wants, that some people starve. Between those two extremes there must be an optimal position.

Having maximized the size of the pie, and having made it grow as fast as possible, it becomes necessary to divide it in such a way as to contribute most to satisfaction. That is, there must be an optimum distribution of income.

You may have noticed that I have not included the prevention of inflation as a separate objective. Logically, avoiding inflation is not a separate objective, but a pre-requisite to the achievement of other objectives. The general level of incomes and prices is of the least possible importance. If, overnight, everyone in the world found his income doubled, and also found that the price of everything he bought was doubled, it would not be of the slightest consequence to him. What happens in inflation, however, is that some incomes do *not* rise as fast as prices; the income distribution is distorted in a way that takes it farther away from the optimum. These distortions in income structure result in turn in misallocation of resources. Even the rate of economic expansion tends to be retarded, especially under conditions of hyper-inflation; rational accounting becomes impossible, investments which seem profitable at the moment turn out to be useless, and a good deal of the plant and equipment acquired turns out to be of the wrong kind when equilibrium is restored. Finally, inflation has hitherto always ended in crisis and depression; the aftermath of inflation is unemployment. Thus violent or cumulative inflation is something that must be eliminated to achieve the other four goals: full employment, optimum distribution of resources, optimum rate of economic expansion, and optimum distribution of income.

Economic Goals and Political Freedoms

Granted my initial value judgments, these objectives are, in themselves, non-controversial. No one who has an open mind could deny that these are worthwhile objectives in themselves. We must try to quantify them, however; and we must ask, "Are these the *sole* objectives of economic policy?"

This brings us to the much-abused question of the relationship between economic goals and political freedoms. Here again the economist has two alternatives. He may leave

the discussion of "freedoms", and the definition of political
goals, to experts in other fields. This approach has certain
advantages. It makes the discussion clear; it distinguishes the
best *economic* policy from the policy that is best *politico-*
economically. The other alternative is for the economist to
make a separate value judgment about political goals. There
is not much harm in this approach, provided the economist
makes his judgments regarding political goals explicit and
clear at the outset. However, economists, as such, know less
about political objectives than they do about economic
objectives. One can *see* how much people want goods and
services, in the market. You can see how much they want
various goods and services by what they are prepared to pay
for them, and the amount they are willing to pay for them
is a fairly clear indication of the relative intensity with
which they desire various goods and services. But economists
do not know very much about people's political aims, especially their valuation of fundamental freedoms. To quote
Dr. Taylor once more:[4]

Political economy is a much broader subject than economic
science; it involves the latter plus all other social or human
sciences, plus philosophical, ethical and political reflection, plus
thoughtful study of human history. And like philosophy, into
which it overlaps, it must forever remain in essential part a
theater of controversy, and never can become entirely a branch
of research leading to agreement on the truth. That is why, as
one of the central controversies in this field, the debate about
the proper spheres of individual freedom and collective control
in the "good" economy is eternally recurrent, wherever thought
and discussion are free.

I am not sure in my own mind just how much people want
"freedom". The businessman, agriculturalist, or trade union
official, when he speaks of his desire for freedom, usually
means "freedom to exploit" — freedom to use his bargaining
power unhampered. But this is not a political freedom; it is
merely one way of expressing a desire for more goods and
services. What they want this freedom for is to use their
bargaining power to increase their share of the national
income. Consequently, the desirability of "freedom to ex-

---

4 O. H. Taylor, *op. cit.,* pp. 641-2.

ploit" can be discussed as part of *economic* policy; it is associated with the general problem of distribution of income.
One could hardly defend "freedom to make the income
distribution worse".

Similarly, I doubt very much whether a typical businessman, farmer, or trade union official, when he stresses the
essentiality of freedom of thought, speech, press and
assembly, is really much concerned with freedom as such.
The test question is, do they want freedom for their
opponents too, or do they want freedom only for themselves?
This is an important question. All governments, and nearly
all people, are quite happy to grant to others the freedom
to express approval of them and agreement with them. In
capitalist countries, the only fundamental issue is: "Shall we
grant these freedoms to Communists?" In the Communist
countries, the only fundamental issue is: "Should there be
freedom of press, of speech, assembly, and so on, for anti-
Communists and pro-capitalists?"

Moreover, even in cases where people want freedom, not
only for themselves but for their opponents, there is still
the question as to what people want freedom for. Very often
people want freedom of press, speech, and the like so that
they will be free to influence governments, directly or
through the electorate, to institute policies that will raise
their share of national income. In this case, "freedom" comes
back once again to the question of income distribution.

For scientists — especially social scientists — the freedom
of thought, speech, and publication, are the heart and soul
of everyday existence. But how much are other people
interested in freedom, apart from the freedom to use any
power they have or can acquire to raise their incomes and
their status? Since I do not know the answer to this question,
I prefer not to make value judgments myself regarding
political goals, and to leave such decisions to the electorate.

Professor Meade neatly distinguishes the position of the
economist in making value judgments about economic goals
and about political aims:[5]

---

[5] James Edward Meade, *Planning and the Price Mechanism*, London, 1948,
p. 38.

Conflicts of judgment about the relative wastes of wealth due, on the one hand, to inequalities of distribution and, on the other hand, to the damage done to economic incentives through measures taken to reduce inequalities, can be reduced by a better scientific examination of the facts of economic life; but conflicts of opinion about the relative desirability of freedom, efficiency, security and equity are conflicts about ultimate values and, in a democratic system, a solution can be sought only through the ballot box. We vote for the type of government which will attach more weight to those of these ultimate ends which, in our opinion, are at the moment too little stressed; and I personally would attach great weight to security and equity as well as to freedom and efficiency.

Like Professor Meade, I am content to let those decisions be made at the ballot box.

Establishing Quantitative Criteria for Policy

We must now try to pin down the objectives of economic policy to a form which, if not measurable, will at least permit recognition of the absence or presence of the situation that is desired. A government has to make four kinds of decisions:

First of all, with regard to full employment without inflation, a government has to decide whether total spending (public and private) should be increased or decreased.

Secondly, with regard to the allocation and distribution of resources among goods and services, four kinds of decisions are required:

(a) How much resources should be allocated to particular goods and services — how much to beer and how much to Bibles?

(b) How much resources should be allocated to public and to private enterprise; in other words, what are the legitimate spheres of public and private enterprise?

(c) How much resources should be used to satisfy wants directly, and how much should be used to satisfy them indirectly by producing goods for export, to exchange for imports?

(d) How much of time should be spent in working (producing goods and services), and how much should be spent in enjoying them (playing)?

Thirdly, the government must decide what share of resources should be used to meet current consumption requirements, and what share for raising future living standards.

Fourthly, it should decide what share of the national income should be allocated to particular occupations, or to particular families.

It is worth noting that governments are already making decisions relative to all these questions, although not always with very clear concepts of them in mind.

Full employment is relatively easy to pin down quantitatively. First, the number of job opportunities must be continuously equal to the number of job-seekers. Secondly, not more than (say) three or four per cent of the working force should be job-seeking at any one time. Full employment does not mean that no one ever has to look for a job. As an economy progresses, some old industries stagnate and die, while some new ones grow up; and this process necessarily involves temporary unemployment. There will always be some people in the process of changing jobs. Finally, no individual worker should be job-seeking for (say) more than two to three months. These criteria are admittedly rules of thumb. Taking three to four per cent rather than two to three per cent or four to five per cent is in some sense arbitrary. However, these figures are based on previous experience, and on estimates of the minimum amount of unemployment needed for maximum economic growth.

If full employment does not exist — that is, if more than four per cent of the working force are unemployed, and if people are remaining unemployed for more than three months — total spending should be increased. If full employment exists (less than three per cent unemployment), and at the same time prices are rising, total spending should be decreased to prevent inflation.

The optimum distribution of resources among goods and services requires that the satisfactions gained by any use of resources should be equal to the satisfaction foregone. Production of beer should be expanded until the satisfaction derived from one more glass of beer is less than the satisfaction derived from something else that could be produced by the same resources. Under certain circumstances, this situation is reflected in the equation of marginal cost — the addition to total costs involved in producing one more glass of beer — to the price of a glass of beer. This criterion applies only if the distribution of income is optimal. Otherwise, prices do not reflect relative social values. For example, if there is a highly unequal income distribution, demand for champagne may be high; a more equal income distribution will reduce the demand for champagne and increase the demand for beer. Also, the equation of marginal cost to price is a satisfactory guide to the distribution of resources only if all units of all factors of production are paid the value of its marginal product (the amount it contributes to total national income). Under conditions of pure competition, there is a tendency for factors of production to be paid at that rate. The cost of producing an additional unit of a commodity then represents the value of all other commodities that could be produced with the same resources. Thus marginal cost becomes a measure of satisfaction foregone. Price is a measure of satisfaction gained. So far, no one has suggested a device for determining whether people prefer more beer or more Bibles better than the market itself — subject to two conditions: that the income distribution is already optimal; and that no firm has power to sell at prices above marginal costs, hire labour at less than value of its marginal product, or buy materials or equipment at less than marginal cost. If the output of every commodity is expanded until the satisfaction gained from one more unit of it is just equal to satisfactions foregone in producing it, the allocation of resources is such that satisfaction is maximized.

Strictly speaking, however, this criterion suffices only for existing firms. No *new* enterprise should be launched unless it appears that the total satisfaction derived from the stream of goods and services it will provide will at least equal the total cost of production, including depreciation of plant and equipment. If this criterion is not met, it will not be worth while sinking resources in that kind of plant and equipment.

As far as possible, the decision with regard to the relative size of public and private sectors should be made in the same way. The public sector — consisting of industries where public enterprise is clearly more efficient than private — should be extended until the satisfactions to be derived from a further public use of resources is equal to the satisfaction to be gained by the most desired private use of the same resources. The only way of determining the location of this point is to compare the cost of public services with what people are willing to pay for them, either as a market price, or as taxes, fees, and the like.

The next question is: How much of resources should be devoted to production for export, and how much should be devoted to producing directly for the home market? Here again, if the foreign exchange rate reflects true differences in relative cost of producing things at home and buying them from abroad, production for export should be expanded so long as the cost of producing and selling another unit is less than the price in the world market.

Finally, with regard to working and playing, the working week should be such that the satisfaction derived from consuming the product of one more hour's work per week is just equal to the satisfaction derived from not working for that hour. If every wage and salary earner is paid the value of his marginal product, this criterion can be met simply by allowing everyone to make his own choice between more work (and thus more income) and more leisure.[6]

When we come to the optimum rate of economic progress, the problem is a bit more difficult. First of all, it is necessary to ask, optimum for whom? I am inclined to argue that governments should consider only the satisfactions of people now alive, including such satisfaction as people now alive get from contemplating the higher standard of living that future generations may have. True, by starving ourselves for the next ten years, our children and grand-children might enjoy a very high standard of living, using the capital that

---

[6] In reality, of course, this choice must be made collectively, because of the interdependence of various occupations, and the difficulty of arranging part-time work.

we had accumulated. But if satisfactions of future generations are rated equally with satisfactions of people now alive, we should be logically compelled to go on starving ourselves, generation after generation, so that when all useful plant, equipment, and inventories had been accumulated, the people then alive would enjoy a colossally high standard of living. Put that way, the absurdity of the proposition is apparent. One might work out a complex system of discounting satisfactions of future generations; but what objective basis could be used except the importance people *now* living attach to the welfare of future generations? The only defensible position is to define "optimum" in terms of people now alive. Of course, the "people now alive" are constantly changing, and the "optimum" may change with them. For this reason, no society should be permitted to be so spendthrift that it fails to maintain its capital and forces on future generations a standard of living actually lower than its own.

The rate of technological progress is not something over which precise control can be exerted by economic policy alone. It depends too much on the growth of knowledge— pure scientific knowledge and engineering knowledge. About all that can be said in this connection is that it is probably a good idea for governments to subsidize research. However, the rate of technological progress also depends on the rate at which discoveries are exploited; in economic parlance, it depends on the rate of *innovation* as well as the rate of *invention*. Now the rate at which new commodities, new techniques, and new resources are developed does depend on economic conditions. What is needed here is an adequate reward for innovation, without permitting the innovator to entrench himself as a monopolist for an unnecessarily long period, or providing opportunities for *retarding* progress by withholding new discoveries from the market.

With regard to the rate of capital accumulation, apart from technological progress, the rule of thumb criterion is that policy should seek to equate the "marginal productivity of capital" with the "marginal rate of time preference". More and more resources should be allocated to increasing the stock of capital, until the increase in total production derived from one more unit of capital (one more machine, say) is not enough to offset the general preference for present consumption over future consumption.

It used to be thought that private enterprise did this job automatically, by equating the rate of capital accumulation to savings at an interest rate which also equated the marginal rate of time preference to the marginal productivity of capital. We now realize that interest rates are only loosely related to volume of saving. Actual market rates of interest are not a very good measure of time preference, and they are not a very good measure of marginal productivity of capital either. Savings and investment are brought into equilibrium, not by movements of the interest rate, but by fluctuations of national income, which may entail inflation or unemployment.

The best one could do would be to estimate marginal productivity of capital in purely technical terms, peg the "pure" rate of interest (rate on government bonds) there, and then equate the volume of public and private investment to the flow of savings forthcoming out of a full employment income. This formula must be modified, however, to allow for the irrationality of people now alive. They tend to underestimate the importance of their *own* future. People now may weigh satisfactions ten years hence rather lightly; but when ten years have gone by, they may wish they had saved more in the past. Governments may need to adopt resource conservation programmes to offset this tendency. Also, there are sometimes specific opportunities for raising the productivity of an economy which private enterprise fails to see or to grasp, and which the government must undertake. Such ventures as the Tennessee Valley Authority, Prairie Farm Rehabilitation Authority or the Snowy River project are unlikely to be undertaken by private enterprise, although the citizens of the countries concerned apparently consider them worth while, in terms of current consumption sacrificed and the increase in the future standard of living they make possible.

Difficulty of Defining Optimal Distribution of Income

Finally, we come to the problem of distribution of income. This is the toughest nut of all to crack. The problem is particularly awkward because, strictly speaking, the decision about income distribution is the *first* that must be made. The best route to the other objectives depends on what income distribution is desired. For example, employment can be increased in depression either by building public low-rental housing projects, or by subsidizing builders to provide houses for the private housing market. If public housing is chosen, the houses are provided to the lower income groups, while the houses built by private enterprise go mainly to the upper income groups. Which of these measures for raising employment is better therefore depends on the society's aims regarding income distribution. Similarly, the flow of savings that will be forthcoming at a given level of national income, which determines the rate of economic expansion, will depend very much on the income distribution. The lower income groups, even today, cannot save very much, while the upper income groups save large proportions of their incomes. The more equally income is distributed, the smaller will be the flow of savings out of a given income at given interest rates, and the slower will be the rate of economic expansion. The optimum distribution of resources depends on the income distribution, because the pattern of costs and prices depends on income. Thus a government — or a society — must make up its mind as to what distribution of income it wants before it selects measures to achieve other objectives.

It has usually been argued that the goal so far as income distribution is concerned should be to maximize the aggregate satisfaction of the society as a whole. If a government accepts that goal, it is required to direct its policy towards equating the "marginal utilities" of individual incomes. That is, it should seek to equate the satisfactions derived from the last shilling of income allocated to every income recipient. Following this criterion means that, if everyone in the economy has identical tastes, and is equally efficient as a "pleasure machine", income must be distributed equally. It also means that if tastes differ, and people vary in efficiency as pleasure machines, income distribution must be made unequal in such a way as to take account of these differences. But then the question arises: "Are not existing differences in tastes, and in ability to enjoy income, the *result* of past inequality of incomes? Are not the refined tastes of the man who enjoys caviar and champagne, and who is unhappy unless he has an original El Greco over his mantel, tastes which anyone could acquire if he had sufficient income to do so?" In deference to this awkward question, it has frequently been argued that the appropriate goal of policy regarding income distribution would be to approach equality gradually, by reserving increases in national income for people in the lower income group. This policy means that it is never necessary to take income away from people; it merely involves giving income to people at the bottom of the income scale. If past rates of technological progress are maintained over a generation or two, substantial equality of income could be achieved in this way.

At this point, however, another awkward question arises: "Do people really get enjoyment out of high incomes because they are high, or only because they are *relatively* high?" Is it the *prestige* attached to larger incomes that counts, rather than the El Greco over the mantel? If everybody had a masterpiece over the mantel — assuming there were enough to go round — would people derive the same satisfaction from them as the few possessors of masterpieces do now?

I am not going to answer this question, because I do not think that the goal of income distribution is to maximize satisfaction anyhow. I am impressed by the argument of the late Professor Henry Simons.[7] He points out that in a competitive economy, without inheritance, where all persons have substantially equal talents for straight thinking, imagination, salesmanship, and chicanery, but are enormously unequal in physical strength . . . the millionaires will be the persons with strong backs.

A dose of Calvinist theology, he adds, would make this

7 Henry C. Simons, *Personal Income Taxation*, Chicago 1938, pp. 12-14.

situation more palatable to the masses; but actually, if a person has been greatly favoured by the Creator in the dispensation of rare physical blessings, it is hard to regard that initial good fortune as a basis for preferential claims against his fellows with respect to scarce goods.

Similarly, one could imagine a world where people, while substantially equal in other respects, display enormously different efficiencies as pleasure machines. Let us imagine also that these efficiencies vary inversely as the cube of the cephalic index. In such a world the criterion of least aggregate sacrifice would require that taxation leave the longheads with very large incomes; and a consistent policy would require that all impecunious longheads be generously subsidized. . . . The criterion implies that the primary objective of policy on earth should be that of generating through the human population the maximum output of pleasure for the contemplation of some external Spectator. . . . A critical, disinterested Spectator would probably conclude, however, that the ethical claims of the longheads were, if anything, weaker and more specious than those of the strongbacks in the other world. If a person obtains a remarkably efficient mechanism for converting income into pleasure, would not a meticulously equitable system equalize as between him and his fellows not marginal or incremental utility but simply total utility?

In other words, rather than say: "We will give this shilling to Joe because he will get more kick out of spending it than Bill would", we should say: "No; I think Joe and Bill should be equally happy, and we will distribute income to ensure that they will be". Now this seems to me a plausible argument. For whose benefit should aggregate satisfaction of society be maximized? If one man is a bed-ridden invalid and another is very healthy, the healthy man certainly can enjoy income more; but it seems a bit rough to say that because a man is bed-ridden, he must also have a lower income. Indeed, maximizing satisfaction is about as sensible as maximizing collective health, which would require the concentration of scarce medical services on people already healthy or who are easily cured, while letting serious and doubtful cases die and chronic cases suffer. Yet, a great deal of economic theory — particularly the theory of public finance — has been built up on the assumption that aggregate satisfaction should be maximized.

All that I am willing to say at this point is that any decision regarding the "optimal" income distribution requires another value judgment; it is not something that economists or anyone else can *know*. It is a matter of "opinion" as to what constitutes the best income distribution. However, I think it is also safe to say that any *defensible* value judgment would require greater equality of income distribution than now exists. At least, the onus of proof is on those who think that the present income distribution, or a still more unequal one, is better than greater equality.

I think, therefore, that there are two alternatives with regard to income distribution. Either the economist can say: "Among the various routes to *other* goals — full employment, and so on — those that make income more equal are better than those that make income distribution more unequal". This is the approach that I find most acceptable. Or the economist can say: "I am willing to accept the opinion of the electorate on the question as to whether incomes should be more equal, and as to how rapidly they should be equalized".

Compatibility of Various Objectives

Are the various objectives mutually consistent, or do they conflict with each other? I think the objectives, properly defined, are not only compatible with each other, but complementary to each other. Full employment is essential to an optimal distribution of resources. Also, full employment is essential to a rapid rate of growth. If an economy wastes resources, it cannot expand as fast as possible. Finally, full employment is consistent with *any* income distribution. Indeed, a society can have any income distribution it likes, and maintain full employment without inflation.

Some people question whether full employment is consistent with the maximum output per man-hour: will not full employment make men lazy? This problem can be handled conceptually by regarding not-working-very-hard as a kind of leisure. If the choice between a lower income and working harder on the job is included as part of the decision between working and playing, there is no conflict between maximizing output per man hour, and full employment; the leisure is part of the total output.

An optimal distribution of resources is essential to the optimal rate of growth. It is consistent with an optimal income distribution, up to the degree of equality that is provided by distributing income according to productivity, giving to everyone that share of the national income which he contributes to it. If greater equality is sought, further re-distribution must be sought through the public fisc rather than through the market. Taxes and subsidies must be used, rather than wages, because differential wage rates are the best means of allocating workers among various occupations in accordance with their relative productivity in different jobs. If workers are paid more than their marginal productivity, unless the surpluses are exactly proportional to the productivity in their various uses, the wage system is no longer an efficient allocator of manpower.

Much the same arguments apply with regard to the allocation of resources between public and private enterprise. No such allocation means much unless full employment prevails. The same is true with regard to the allocation between production for home and foreign markets.

As to the decision of work *versus* play, since full employment is defined in terms of this decision, full employment means that everybody is able to work who wants to do so at the prevailing wage, and for the working week which represents his own choice between more income and more leisure or, more realistically, which represents the choice made by the majority of members of his trade union. The length of the working week should be the unions' decision, by the way, and nobody else's. If the optimum position is to be attained, the employer should influence the length of the working week only by the amount of real wages he offers for more work.[8]

A high rate of technological progress helps to maintain full

8 A colleague raises this question: Suppose the supply curve of labour in an industry is backward sloping, so that offering higher wages *reduces* the labour offered, while consumers want more of the commodity? I would stand by my statement even then; but it might be desirable to offer special incentives for extra work.

employment, by providing investment outlets. It also increases the flow of final products, so that its effect need not be inflationary in the long run.

The optimum rate of capital accumulation is defined in terms of the optimum income distribution. Therefore, there is no conflict between these two objectives. True, greater equality of income will tend to reduce the rate of economic expansion. This fact does not constitute a conflict, however, because a society must decide *first* what the optimum income distribution is, and *then* determine the optimum rate of expansion in terms of that income distribution. Thus there appears to be no fundamental conflict among the major objectives.

How to Attain Economic Goals

It remains to say something about how to attain these objectives. I have no particular programme to sell, nor can I assess the relative merits of various proposals in the compass of half a lecture. The literature on economic policy fills shelves. All that I can do is to indicate the *kind* of measure that is involved. I need do no more for my purpose here, which is to indicate why conflict arises in connection with the selection and execution of these policies.

(1) *Full employment without inflation*: It seems advisable to begin by introducing as much flexibility into the fiscal system as possible. A government should make as much use as possible of those devices which automatically increase the income stream when it tends to fall, and reduces it when it tends to rise. Unemployment insurance is such a device; benefits go up when unemployment is increasing and go down when unemployment is decreasing. A highly progressive tax structure has a similar effect. When incomes rise, tax collections go up more than proportionately, and impose a brake on expansion. When incomes fall, tax collections fall in greater proportion, thus providing a partial offset to the initial contraction in spending. Payroll taxes are especially flexible. Payroll taxes go down when unemployment is increasing, and rise when unemployment is decreasing.

Secondly, to help stabilize consumption, devices such as family allowances and consumer subsidies are useful.

Thirdly, a counter-cyclical public investment policy is essential; government expenditures on goods and services—particularly capital goods — should vary inversely with the level of private spending.

Fourthly, tax rates and structures should be varied in a counter-cyclical fashion. Tax rates should be raised in inflation and cut in depression. In addition, in so far as is administratively feasible, government should shift from one type of tax to another, according to the general economic situation. A tax on spending is a good thing in inflation, but a bad thing in depression; a capital tax is a good thing in a depression, but a bad thing in inflation; the same is true of an undistributed profits tax.

Finally, government stockpiling schemes, and encouragements to private enterprise to stabilize employment through stockpiling and dovetailing, are desirable adjuncts of an all-out attack on inflation and unemployment.

(2) *Optimal distribution of resources*: The achievement of an optimal distribution of resources also requires an integrated programme, utilizing a variety of measures. Despite grave limitations, American and Canadian experience indicates that anti-trust legislation helps to check the formation of monopolies. Tax-and-bounty schemes can be used to persuade natural monopolists to behave as though they were not. In effect, these schemes involve paying monopolists to increase their output to a competitive level, and then taxing (super-normal profits plus subsidies) away from them. In some instances public regulation of monopolies, including price control, may be desirable. Sometimes public ownership is called for, either through appropriating private interests, or by setting up competing public concerns. The vexed question of wage control is involved too; if wages are to be used to allocate labour, relative wage rates must be proportional to productivity. Some control over the location of industry, so that industries will be established where they will be most productive, is also desirable.

(3) *Optimal rate of economic progress*: I have already suggested subsidization of research to stimulate invention. Secondly, patent laws should be revised; the period of pro-

tection under present patent laws seems unnecessarily long, especially since patent lawyers find it so easy to get patents renewed. Third, monetary policy should maintain interest rates at the marginal productivity level. In order to overcome irrationality and lack of foresight on the part of private investors, soil conservation, town, country, and regional planning, and national development programmes should be undertaken.

Conclusions

These are the things which I think I have demonstrated:

First — that unambiguous and non-controversial objectives of economic policy can be defined.

Second — that, except for the optimum distribution of income, these objectives can be cast in terms which are either measurable or recognizable.

Third — that the objectives are mutually consistent.

Fourth — that policies can be formulated to achieve these objectives.

It is worthy of note that these policies are not inconsistent with freedoms of thought, speech, press, assembly or election. Moreover, they allow people to spend their incomes as they like, and choose their own occupations. The policies *are*, however, inconsistent with the "freedom to exploit".

If these things are true, why don't we go right ahead and instrument these policies? There are two reasons. One is misunderstanding. The other is lack of good-will. We do not live in societies comprised uniquely of well-informed men of good-will. Many people, while admitting that these may be legitimate objectives for society as a whole, nevertheless say in their actual social and political life, "Well, that is all very well for *society*, but *I* would rather have higher profits (or higher wages)". In other words, there are powerful individuals and groups operating in their own interest, against the national interest. The result is social conflict as to the type of economic policy which should be adopted.

IV

ECONOMICS, SOCIAL CONFLICT, AND WAR

IN THE PREVIOUS LECTURE I contended that, given three plausible value judgments, it is possible to state objectives of economic policy which are unambiguous and non-controversial. I then suggested the general nature of the policies that would be required to meet those objectives, and indicated that the policies are perfectly consistent with freedoms of speech, press, assembly and election, and also with free choice of occupation and free choice in the distribution of one's own income. But they are not consistent with the "freedom to exploit"; that is, the freedom to use bargaining power to the full. Economic conflict arises mainly from the exercise of the freedom to exploit, and current political conflict is largely a reflection of economic conflict.

By economic conflict I mean conflict concerning the production and distribution of goods and services. This conflict may be either subjective or objective; that is to say, individuals or groups may *believe* that they have a community of interest, in opposition to the interests of other individuals or groups, concerning the production and distribution of goods and services. In that case the conflict would be subjective. Beyond that, there may in fact be a community of interest which is in conflict with the interests of other groups. In that case there would be an objective conflict as well.

The most obvious form of conflict concerns the distribution of income among individuals and groups. However, there is another kind of conflict which is extremely important, and which I think should be included under the heading of economic conflict; the struggle for *power to control* the production and distribution of goods and services, or power to make the fundamental decisions regarding the production and distribution of goods and services.

There may also be conflicts over the objectives of economic policy. Not everyone would accept the value judgments laid down in the preceding lecture. Not all individuals or groups express goodwill in their economic and political activities.

84

For example, there is a wide difference of opinion among workers and employers as to how full "full employment" should be as an objective of policy.

Finally, there may be conflict over the selection of specific measures for the achievement of objectives, even when agreement on objectives exists.   .

Is Economic Conflict "Class" Conflict?

A good deal of time and effort has been spent in discussing whether or not economic conflict is "class" conflict. I do not consider this discussion very important, since it is largely a debate over definitions. Under nineteenth century capitalism, when the distribution of property, of income, of political power, and of social status roughly coincided, there was indeed a fairly clear-cut *class* conflict between the owners of means of production (land and capital) and people who were hired to work with them. Today, however, these class lines are becoming blurred. With the growth of powerful trade unions, farmers' co-operatives, labour governments and the like, ownership, income, and political power are tending to diverge. For example, one can find many poor farmer-owners who, from the standpoint of income or political power, or even of social prestige, are in a lower class than the highly skilled worker. Moreover, there are many economic conflicts which are not clearly "class" conflicts. For example, manufacturers may find themselves in conflict with primary producers over tariffs on importations of raw materials. There might even be conflict between the publishers of newspapers and the domestic newsprint industry, over the rate of tariff which should be applied to imported newsprint. There is growing evidence that workers in the monopolistic industries are not above helping their employers to exploit consumers, in the hope of sharing in monopoly gains through higher wages. In Australia we have recently been treated to the spectacle of a conflict between members of certain trade unions on the one hand, and a Labour government and a Council of Trade Unions on the other.

While recognizing the difficulty of drawing sharp class lines so far as economic conflicts are concerned, it is nevertheless possible to distinguish, in the Western democracies, three major power groups, which I shall call "Big Business", "Big Labour", and "Big Agriculture". These groups are bound by a common economic interest, and they operate politically, sometimes having political parties of their own, as in Australia, where the Liberal Party, Labor Party and Country Party each reflect the special interests of one particular group, and sometimes relying on powerful lobbies, as in the United States.

Is the conflict among these groups economic? The extreme view — which has been expressed even by so distinguished a social scientist as Professor Frank Knight — is that conflict among such groups is scarcely economic at all:

Reflection will reveal that it is rather an accident that internal social conflicts take the economic form. This will be clear if one pictures the situation which would result if every adult were granted the power to work physical miracles, and could bring about any desired physical result simply by wishing, thus eliminating all problems of production and distribution. Problems of associative life would then arise only in the other two of the three main forms of interest and activity we have recognized, i.e., in play and culture. But without some revolutionary change in human nature, conflicts in these fields would be as acute as those to which economic interests give rise, and they would not be essentially different in form. It is probable that the necessity of economic activity and co-operation actually reduces social conflict on the whole.[1]

Very few economists indeed share this view. There are, however, a number of economists who would contend that *objective* economic conflict would disappear under conditions of pure competition. This view had its historical origin in the remarks of Adam Smith about the invisible hand which guides us in the pursuit of our selfish interests to promote social welfare. It found its most austere statement in the works of J. B. Clark, which purported to show "scientifically" that pure competition would guarantee a socially optimal economic situation. More recently, it has been reiterated by such "latter-day laissez-faire" economists as Professor Lionel Robbins:[2]

---

[1] Frank W. Knight and Thornton W. Merriam, *The Economic Order and Religion*, London 1947, p. 78.
[2] *The Economic Basis of Class Conflict*, London 1939, p. 7.

The clue to a successful approach to the problem, as I see it, lies in the analysis of markets. In the exchange society, the market is, as it were, the reflection of the whole network of economic relationships. . . . If, for instance, peasant producers are confronted with a single buyer or a small number of buyers acting in concert, they may feel that their interests are damaged by such conditions; and very often they will be right. Similarly, if they buy their implements from a monopoly or if they borrow money from a closed group of money-lenders, there will exist a like community of interest. . . . The only sense which the economist can attach to the term exploitation of labour is as a description of what happens where a group of competing workers is confronted by a monopolistic buyer. . . . When the conditions of supply and demand are such as either to confront buyers and sellers with monopolistic organizations or to permit buyers or sellers themselves to act as groups, then the objective conditions of conflict are present.

The implication here is that *only* under monopolistic conditions are objective causes of economic conflict present. Now, there is *some* sense in this argument. Under conditions of pure competition — which means that no firm is big enough, relative to the industry as a whole, to exert any influence on the prices of things it buys or of the prices of things it sells — the maximum-profit output of existing firms usually approximates very closely to the socially optimal output as well, for a given level of employment and a given distribution of income. Pure competition also assures that adjustments to changes in tastes and in costs will be in the right direction and reasonably prompt. Very important is the fact that, under pure competition there are no wasteful "selling costs"; that is, no high-pressure advertising, no expensive packaging, no suave salesmen in morning coats and striped trousers, and the other unessentials of modern marketing. No one has ever heard a "blurb" on the wireless to the effect that Farmer Brown's brand of number-one-northern-hard-red-wheat is more healthful and invigorating than anybody else's number-one-northern-hard-red-wheat. Where you have highly standardized commodities being sold by very large numbers of sellers, as you have in wheat and cotton and similar world markets, you have pure competition, and you have no advertising. Under pure competition, moreover, there is no "exploitation" of factors of production, in the sense of paying less than the value of their marginal product; each factor of production withdraws from the national income what it contributes to it. Finally, only "normal" profits can be earned — profits just high enough to make it worth while for a businessmen to stay in his particular field.

There is also a good deal of nonsense in the argument. First of all, it is clear that incomes can still be very unequal under pure competition because of differences in inherited wealth or inherited productive capacity. In the previous lecture, I mentioned Professor Simons' argument that where all people are identical in all other talents but different in physical strength under pure competition, the millionaires will be the people with the strong backs; and pointed out that it is hard to argue that those people born healthier than others should also be richer than others. There is very little relationship between individual merit and income, even in a purely competitive society.

"Normal" profits, moreover, may be very high, especially if the interest, rents, and withdrawals components of entrepreneurial income are included. Normal profits of a risky competitive enterprise may very well be higher than profits in a cosy, well-entrenched monopoly which is nevertheless subject to competition from firms producing close substitutes — a situation which economists will recognize as Chamberlin's "tangency case". Risk valuations may be excessive, or "safety-preference" too high; that is, entrepreneurs in the fields may be over-reluctant to gamble. And is not "normal" profit really an "accustomed" normal? Is it not something that can change? I see little evidence of a wholesale exodus from Australia's pastoral industries — which are about as competitive as any — because of the increase in income tax over recent years. Normal profit may be excessive even apart from risk valuations. It is conceivable, for example, that a civil servant might run a business just as well as the present entrepreneur, and accept a salary lower than the "normal" profit, because the civil servant is more thoroughly imbued with the ideal of public service than the business man.

Finally, inequality of income also leads to inequality of opportunity, and even Professor Robbins admits that inequality of opportunity is particularly hard to justify. The rich man has better opportunities than the poor man for acquiring additional training and for exploiting profitable investment opportunities. Particularly difficult to countenance is the fact that, under pure competition, people who are very rich will be paid for being very rich; that is to say, they will be receiving interest on their savings, and their savings will reflect mainly the fact that they are too rich to spend all their incomes.

Nor is the allocation of resources under pure competition *necessarily* and *exactly* optimal. For instance, if entrepreneurs misjudge the objective risks of investment outlets, resources will not be perfectly allocated. Entrepreneurs in the Canadian wheat industry may under-estimate or over-estimate the chance of an early frost in the northern part of the prairie provinces. If they under-estimate it, and cultivate those parts, there will be a waste of resources; if they over-estimate it, and fail to cultivate them, fertile lands will be left undeveloped without reason. If firms go bankrupt through bad guesses, it is not only the entrepreneur who suffers; employees, consumers, and indeed the whole community, suffer a loss in the form of unduly high frictional unemployment and wasted fixed resources. It is true, of course, that the entrepreneur in the strict sense of the term "pays" for the fixed factors (land and capital) used. But the entrepreneur is willing to pay only the discounted sum of the income received from the asset during its life; the value of the asset to society would be something in excess of that, because the asset also raises the productivity of the labour with which it is combined. If the asset turns out to be useless, there is therefore a loss to society as well as to the investor.

It is even more doubtful whether pure competition would guarantee an optimal rate of economic expansion. The current marginal cost, as it appears to the entrepreneur, may not measure the social cost of depleting natural resources. We have inherited from the competition of the past a legacy of exhausted soils, dust-bowls, mined forests, ghost towns, and the like. Nor does pure competition guarantee foresight and daring in entrepreneurs. Some projects, such as the Tennessee Valley Scheme or the Snowy River project, may be too large or too risky to be undertaken by the small firms that would exist under pure competition. There is even some question as to whether economic expansion would take place at all under continuous pure competition. Professor Schumpeter has presented cogent arguments for the thesis that the mainspring of economic expansion under capitalism is the hope of at least temporary monopoly profits for entrepreneurs who are first in a new field.

Finally, pure competition does not guarantee full employment without inflation. Pure competition in the capital market does not guarantee that investment will equal savings at full employment levels of national income. At the very least, Professor Schumpeter's "two-phase cycle", comprising inflationary boom and a return to full employment equilibrium, may occur in pure competition. The effect of pure competition on the level of employment, even when defined to include complete price-cost flexibility, is still a matter of controversy among economists. My own conclusion is that the one thing that complete flexibility of all prices and costs assures is that the level of employment and of unemployment will tend to stay where it is. It does not in itself assure a return to full employment if unemployment prevails.

In the real world, there is a more or less continuous gradation of monopoly power from one firm, co-operative, and union to another. Is it not absurd to suppose that economic conflict disappears completely in precisely those areas of the economy in which elasticity of demand and supply of everything is zero for all bargaining units — that is, in the areas where no monopoly power exists, and no individual, firm, union, or other organization can have any effect on the prices of the thing it buys or of the thing it sells?

Intensification of Conflict by Monopoly Exploitation

Under the monopoly conditions of the real world, there is additional conflict, in the sense that prices are above marginal costs, that profits may be higher than normal and wages below value of marginal product, and in the sense that the level of output is less than the socially optimal output. Under conditions where only selling monopolies exist, there would not be much *political* conflict, unless and until consumers or workers became organized. The chief problem in a world divided into a small number of power groups is not so much that economic conflict is enhanced, as it is that economic conflict becomes translated into social and political conflict. For example, under pure monopsony in the labour market (one or a few employers faced with large numbers of competing workers) there is an objective conflict of economic interest between the employer and the employee. Workers will be paid less than the value of their marginal product, employers will receive more than the value of their marginal product. The *political* conflict, however, is obviously greater when the workers no longer bargain as individuals, but are organized into strong trade unions. Yet under bilateral monopoly (a monopolistic seller faced by a monopsonistic buyer), the case most frequently found in the labour market today, bargaining power might very well be equal, and the rates of wages and profits that result could be exactly the same as they would be under pure competition. But it would be ridiculous to say that under these conditions there is no more conflict than there would be under pure competition. The fact that powerful employers' organizations are confronted by equally powerful trade unions gives rise to an immense amount of social and political conflict, irrespective of the outcome so far as wages and profits are concerned.

In a world of monopolies in which bargaining power is equally distributed, the general equilibrium could be exactly the same as would occur under pure competition; the degree of misallocation of resources and maldistribution of income would be less than under the conditions of pure monopoly. Yet a world of monopolies would be a world of intense conflict. When an economy is organized into three major groups, political conflict becomes especially intense.

Types of Economic Conflict

It is important in this connection to distinguish conflict over the distribution of income from conflict over status. It is also essential to distinguish conflict over objectives from conflict over measures for achieving them. The failure to make these distinctions has led Professor Knight into what seems to me an egregious error:[3]

> By far the most serious problem arises out of the tendency of a market economy under real conditions to fall into oscillatory changes of cycles of expansion and contraction. These occur in most fields of production, but of course the main source of hardship and insecurity is the alternation of boom and depression in economic life as a whole, which is known as "the business cycle". Only two observations can be made about this phenomenon here. The first is that practically no one profits by it; hence conflicts of interest are not a factor in the problem. Remedial action is a matter of scientific understanding and political and administrative competence.

This view fails to recognize that there are different routes to the elimination of the business cycle, with different effects upon the distribution of income among workers, farmers, and businessmen. For example, inflation could be checked either by price ceilings, rationing, and taxes on the higher incomes, or by wage ceilings, spending taxes, and the payment of a high rate of interest on savings bonds. The effect on the income distribution as between the lower and the upper income groups is exactly the reverse under the two programmes. Similarly, one could approach the unemployment problem by public housing programmes plus family allowances, or by a subsidized private building programme. The effect on the income distribution is the opposite in the two cases. One could meet the dollar shortage by the payment of export subsidies which, in this country, would help mainly the agricultural groups, or by restricting importations of capital goods, which would conflict with the interests of manufacturers, or by restricting imports of American movies and magazines, which would militate mainly against those in

---

[3] F. H. Knight and T. W. Merriam, *The Economic Order and Religion*, London 1947, p. 84.

the lower income group. Naturally, conflict arises over the selection of routes to any objective.

There can also be conflict with regard to the effect on status of different routes to full employment without inflation. The antagonism of American big business and finance to the New Deal was much less a matter of feeling that the policies which it proposed would reduce their incomes than it was of feeling that it would destroy their prestige and status, by introducing policies executed and administered by government officials, as distinct from policies executed and administered by businessmen and financiers. The social significance of the New Deal was that it shifted responsibility for the major decisions regarding the production and distribution of goods and services from businessmen to government officials; that is the thing for which the business and financial community never forgave President Roosevelt.

Inflation and Unemployment as Causes of Conflict

Surely inflation and unemployment are among the major causes of social conflict. Anyone who doubts the importance of unemployment as a source of social conflict should recall the hunger marches on London and Washington during the great depression, the police and militia firing into crowds of angry and embittered workers, the threatened revolutions, the actual development of Fascism in Italy, Spain and Germany during the primary and secondary post-war depressions, and the war that followed. No one could say for sure just what upheavals would come out of another great depression — a depression which could be, in the absence of appropriate policies to prevent it, as much greater than the great depression of the thirties as World War II was greater than World War I — but that some social upheavals would result is certain.

Inflation, too, disrupts social stability. In such countries as Germany, France and Italy, memories of the horrors of hyper-inflation were still so fresh in the 'thirties that many people considered even mass unemployment a lesser evil than inflation. Policies to relieve unemployment were rejected

simply because they *might* lead to inflation. In a country that
has seen its price level rise over a billion-fold, observed a life-
time's savings wiped out overnight, the middle class destroyed
and the working class impoverished, social conflict is greatly
intensified, and conditions are created which enable radical
parties of right or left to come to power.

One might, however, ask whether the conflict arising from
inflation and unemployment is subjective or objective. It is
subjective in the sense that no major group can benefit from
unemployment or inflation in the long run. But it is objective in the sense that the optimal degree of unemployment
and the optimal degree of inflation under a given politico-
social framework is different for labour, for agriculture and
for business. It is also objective in the sense that different
policies affect the major power groups differently regarding
the distribution of income and prestige. Thus, big business
in the United States of America stresses "built-in flexibility",
or automatic devices for maintaining full employment without inflation, which they hope will make it unnecessary for
government officials to make decisions affecting the production and distribution of goods and services. They also emphasize the desirability of employment stabilization by
private enterprise. Organizations like the Committee for
Economic Development endeavour to instill into American
business an expansionist philosophy, which will minimize
the role of the government in maintaining full employment
without inflation. All this is part of the general struggle of
American enterprise to regain its pre-1929 status, and to
recapture its *control* over the operation of the American
economy. Thus examination of the facts reveals keen conflict
among major groups regarding full employment without
inflation.

International Economic Conflict

Let us turn now to the international aspects of economic
conflict. To what extent is international conflict — especially
war — the result of economic causes? By "cause", we must
mean something which induces politically powerful groups
to persuade their governments to go to war. Professor Robbins, in another of his writings, suggests that one might say

that the "cause" of World War I was the telegram from Sarajevo conveying the news of the assassination of Archduke Ferdinand. That telegram was only a proximate cause. When we think of political, social and economic causes, we must be thinking of something which induces powerful groups to exert pressure on governments. If the cause is to be economic, the "something" must have to do with the production and distribution of goods and services. Politically powerful groups must think either that they will achieve higher incomes from war, or that they will increase their *control* over the production and distribution of goods and services through war, and thus enhance their status.

According to Marxist doctrine, all wars are economically caused. The state is the creature of the ruling capitalist class; in an effort to offset the declining rate of profit, this dominant capitalist class leads its government into war — particularly colonial conquest — to acquire new sources of raw materials, new markets for finished goods, new opportunities for profitable investment, and new outlets for population pressure. At the opposite pole is the "latter-day *laissez-faire*" view, which says that international conflict arises out of monopoly and restrictions on trade and immigration. If all barriers to free international movement of men, money, and goods were removed, the argument proceeds, international conflict — or at least the objective basis of it — would disappear.

Let us examine these arguments in reverse order. Imagine, first of all, a world in which all governments maintain full employment without inflation, in which there is a complete absence of monopolies, where all men and resources move quickly and without cost into the occupations where they are most productive, and in which there is complete freedom of trade and immigration. In such a world no nation could be better off than another by virtue of its superior natural wealth, since people and capital would move to those countries where their productivity was highest, until the marginal productivity of a given kind of resource was equalized throughout the world.

Under these conditions international economic conflict

would be reduced to a very low level. True, even under these conditions, one nation, having no more natural wealth than another, might nevertheless be richer by virtue of harder work or higher managerial skill; but such extra richness could scarcely be begrudged.

Where there are restrictions upon immigration, this happy state of affairs no longer exists. Then even people with equal willingness and ability to work will get different real incomes according to the wealth and natural resources of the countries in which they happen to live. Moreover, the differences will be cumulative, because the richer nations will be better able to save, and so accumulate capital equipment that will raise their productivity still higher. Under these conditions, the under-privileged countries will turn envious eyes on their more fortunate neighbours, and international economic conflict will arise.

If there are also restrictions upon freedom of trade, the conflict is intensified. For so long as there is freedom of trade, the raw materials and products of the world are obtainable by people of all countries on equal money terms, even if some people have to do more work than others to get a certain amount of money, by virtue of their living in less wealthy countries. Anyone who can and will pay the price, regardless of where he lives, can buy any raw material or finished goods. Likewise, anyone can sell his output in any market whatsoever, provided he is willing to sell at a price as low as his competitors, no matter from what country he comes.

In any market where there are many competing sellers, no one of them can raise the price he gets by restricting his supply. Where there are many competing buyers, no one of them can lower the price he pays by withholding his demand. Similarly, it pays a political unit to restrict its demand for or supply of a particular commodity only if its share in total demand or supply in the world market is a large one. Only then can it get a better price by such restriction. It is only natural that large political units, like the British Empire, Russia, the United States, and the French Empire, will find more opportunities for exploitation of special advantages within the areas under their sovereignty than small units. Consequently, international animosity is directed primarily against countries that are large markets or large producers.

Restrictionism in the field of international trade got its first impetus in the "mercantilist" period of the seventeenth century. Today, the arguments advanced by pressure groups interested in getting protection for their particular products are not so very different from the arguments presented by the mercantilists: the need for large stocks of precious metals as a basis for monetary expansion or for a war chest; the need to give protection to "infant industries"; the need to protect the standard of living from "cheap foreign labour", and so forth.

When restrictions upon trade are imposed, some peoples are able to obtain goods more cheaply than others even in money terms; and some are able to sell more advantageously than others. If a tariff is imposed by one country against some foreign commodity, consumers in the country imposing the tariff pay more for the commodity than otherwise; and the foreign producers now have to add the tariff on to their costs, and they profit less by selling at a given price than they did before the tariff was imposed. That means that they in turn must sell more of their own goods, in order to get enough exchange to pay for a given amount of goods produced by the country imposing the tariff. The imposition of a tariff against the goods that foreigners sell, say, in the United States, is in effect a rise in the price to them of the goods they buy in the United States. Of course, if tariffs against the goods of a particular country are higher than the tariffs against the same goods of another country, the ability of the people of the country discriminated against to buy goods is reduced still more relative to other countries, and economic conflict is even more intense.

Monopolization involves restricting supplies and raising prices, and also paying the factors of production hired less than the value of their contribution to the production of the monopolized industry. Monopolies exploit domestic and foreign consumer alike; but when a particular country has a monopoly of a certain product, foreign consumers suffer by having to pay higher prices, and have to sacrifice a larger amount of their own product to obtain the desired foreign product. Monopoly enhances international economic conflict.

The lack of free and costless mobility of labour and capital, combined with the imperfect ability of entrepreneurs to foresee economic conditions, raises still louder clamours for "protection against unfair foreign competition", to which governments, made nervous by growing unrest, usually yielded.

International Conflict and World Resources

If all countries were identically blessed with natural resources, international restrictions on trade, immigration, and competition would not be of much consequence. If each country were rich in a few important resources, all equally desired, lack of international trade would be disastrous for all, and would therefore be less likely to give rise to conflict. The gains from international trade would be too apparent. Unfortunately, the distribution of natural resources is unequal both as to quantities and as to qualities of raw materials found within the sovereignty of different governments. According to a prewar study of the Royal Institute of International Affairs, "The three best-endowed political units in the world are the United States, the U.S.S.R., and the British Empire. Of these the British Empire is strikingly deficient in petroleum and cotton, the U.S.S.R. in rubber, tin, bauxite, and nickel, and the United States in rubber, tin, manganese, and nickel, to name only the major gaps in each case."[4] The British Empire produced 99.5 per cent of the world's jute, 94 per cent of its nickel, 58 per cent of its rubber, 51 per cent of its wool, 44.5 per cent of its lead, 30 per cent of its copper, 25 per cent of its coal, 24 per cent of its cotton, 23 per cent of its wheat, 20.5 per cent of its vegetable oils. The United States and the U.S.S.R. were almost as well supplied.

"In the case of France, Germany, Italy, and Japan," says the Royal Institute, "the deficiencies are so numerous that it is better to examine such resources as they do possess." Of

---

[4] *Raw Materials and Colonies*, Information Department Paper Number 18.

these four, France was clearly the best supplied, having abundant iron, and a sufficiency of flax, nickel, and vegetable oils. Italy had silk, hemp, minor metals, and vegetable oils. Germany was deficient in everything but coal and potash, and possibly timber. Japan had silk, sulphur, coal, and copper, but was seriously deficient in iron and other textiles. Raw cotton alone accounted for over 30 per cent of Japanese imports. It is worth noting that an economic bloc composed of Japan, China, and Manchukuo would have been much more self-sufficient than Japan alone.

The British Empire, the United States, and the U.S.S.R. were almost self-sufficient in foodstuffs. Due to the peculiar nature of her diet, which consisted mainly of rice, fish, and soya beans, Japan was also virtually self-sufficient in foodstuffs. Japan was still very largely an agricultural nation, nearly half the population being engaged in agriculture. Germany and Italy, on the other hand, were largely dependent upon imports for their foodstuffs.

It is clear that such a situation was bound to give rise to conflict in a world where freedom of trade and freedom of immigration did not exist. Small wonder that the "have-nots" have been loud in their demands for territorial expansion.

The Demands of the "Have-Nots"

In the main, the demand of the "have-nots" for new territory has been based upon arguments, strongly reminiscent of the Marxist doctrine of imperialist wars:

1. These countries need room for a growing population.
2. They must have access to raw materials and markets.
3. They must have outlets for investment.

Let us examine these arguments one by one.

(a) *Population Pressure.* In October of 1918, Colonel House, who was Wilson's collaborator in the presentation of the famous "fourteen points", publicly acknowledged Germany's need for *Lebensraum*. The need for "living-space" has been reiterated by German spokesmen ever since. Japan used the population pressure argument to justify the invasion of Manchuria and later of China. Italy used it to justify the invasion of Ethiopia.

It must be admitted that it is indeed possible for a country to have too large a population, in the sense that the point of "diminishing returns" to increasing labour force has been passed, and the per capita income would be higher if the population were smaller. In new countries, the population may well be too small in this same sense; but Germany, Italy, and Japan quite clearly do not belong in this category. Even in old countries, a growing population may have a beneficial effect on per capita income, by providing the basis for heavy investment in housing, transportation, public utilities, and so forth. However, these beneficial effects can be obtained as well or better if the population grows from a low level as from a high one, and can also be obtained in other ways.

The situation with respect to concentration of population is indicated by the following table:

Density of Population per Square Mile of Arable Land

Japan	2,774
United Kingdom	2,170
Belgium	1,709
Italy	819
Germany	806
France	467
U.S.A.	229

SOURCE: *China and Japan*, Royal Institute of International Affairs, Information Pamphlet Number 21, page 87.

It would be erroneous, however, to argue merely from the fact that England had more people per square mile of arable land than either Germany or Italy, that the "population pressure" arguments of the latter countries were without foundation. The number of people a country can support depends upon the wealth of natural resources available to it, directly and through trade; upon the amount of capital available for investment; upon the level of technique and skill; and upon the terms of trade. On these grounds, it seems possible that Germany and Italy, and certainly Japan, were indeed at a relative disadvantage with respect to the size of their populations. It is worth noting that whereas population in Germany, France, and England was well-nigh stationary,

Japanese population was still growing at the rate of one million a year.

It does not follow from these facts alone that the demands of the "have-nots" for territorial expansion — especially for colonies — were justified. If freedom of immigration prevailed, people could move from over-populated countries to under-populated countries, and the problem would be solved. Before World War I, such movements took place on a large scale. Indeed, in 1914, there were more Germans and Italians in New York City than there were in the German and Italian colonies. Before World War II there were more Japanese in Brazil, Hawaii, and U.S.A. than in Manchukuo. But today the situation is different. The American quota laws of 1921 and 1926, and similar immigration restrictions in Canada, Australia and other countries, virtually closed much of the new world to immigrants of many nationalities. Under these conditions, population pressure constitutes a real problem for the "have-nots".

(b) *Raw Materials and Markets.* The need for raw materials and the need for markets are usually presented as separate reasons for demanding new territory. If markets for finished goods are available, the foreign exchange for purchase of raw materials is available. The "have-nots" were prevented from buying raw materials of other countries only to the extent that they were prevented from selling their own products on favourable terms. Indeed, since favourable terms of trade enable a country to support a larger population, all three arguments — population pressure, need for raw materials, need for markets — are closely related.

It is a mistake to suppose that transfer of sovereignty over any particular territory — say the former German colonies — involves in and of itself a transfer of ownership of raw materials. Apart from outright expropriation of the present holders of private property, which was not the official plan of the "have-nots", raw materials have to be paid for just the same as before. Nor does it matter if the "have-nots" are able to circulate their own currency in the territory trans ferred to them; in the absence of exchange control such an increase in their monetary circulation would merely cause a decline in the value of their currency on the world market, thus raising the price to them of all imports. True, this depreciation in their currency may lead to a temporary increase in exports, but that effect could be obtained by straight-forward devaluation, and has nothing to do with territorial demands.

This is not to deny that transfer of sovereignty may not alleviate the shortage of raw materials of the "have-nots". For, having new territory under their dominion, they can prevent the people living in those territories from buying goods from other countries, and compel them to buy their own goods. In this manner an improved market for their own output is obtained, making it easier for them to pay for the needed raw materials. As generations go by and people in the territories acquired develop tastes for the products of the "fatherland", and perhaps a sense of loyalty to the fatherland, it may be possible to sell goods there on favourable terms even apart from restrictions upon imports from elsewhere.

(c) *The Need for New Fields for Investment.* Some hundred and twenty-five years ago Malthus, and about half a century later Mill, suggested that the only field left for large-scale expansion of investment was foreign trade and the exploitation of new countries. Marx had a similar idea, and argued that international competition for new investment fields in the struggle to avoid falling profits would lead to imperialistic wars. Today in advanced capitalist countries we hear much about declining investment opportunities, economic "maturity", and the consequent "secular stagnation".

On the other hand, excess savings and the need for outlets for investment can hardly be said to have characterized the situation of the "have-nots" since the first world war, or even since 1929. Japan, Italy, and Germany, under the impetus of rapid rearmament, felt rather a lack of investment funds, and were compelled to resort to foreign borrowing or some species of inflation to finance their expansion. It was the "haves" that were bothered by lack of investment outlets and secularly falling profits. Thus, while the argument has a sound logical foundation, it does not apply to the actual conditions of the under-privileged nations during the period when their demands for new territories were most vociferous.

(d) *The "Colonial" Aspect of the Demands of the Have-nots.* While there is some justification for the demands of the "have-nots" for territorial or trade concessions, the case for the need for colonies is less clear. According to the Report of the League Committee on Raw Materials in 1937, "The total present production of all commercially important raw materials in all colonial territories is no more than about 3 per cent of world production." The great bulk of raw materials production is carried on in sovereign states.

Nor have colonies played so great a role in release of population pressure as have sovereign states. Of the 13 million people in the German colonies in 1914, after thirty years of German occupation, only 25,000 were Germans. Italy settled only 25,000 people in Libya in twenty-five years, most of them being soldiers stationed there. The number of Italian labourers in Italian East Africa actually fell from 115,000 in March of 1937 to 21,000 in July 1938; the men were too badly needed at home for military preparation! Similarly, of the 34 million people in Manchuria before World War II, Japan had settled only half a million Japanese despite forty years of occupation. Thus it is clear that colonial accessions are much less important to the "have-nots" than accessions of sovereign states. On the other hand, it must be recognized that under present conditions, when other markets are closed to their goods and other countries are closed to their emigrants, colonies may well play a much bigger role than they have in the past.

In the real world, a basis for international economic conflict exists. The conflict becomes especially intense during periods of hyper-inflation or deep unemployment. During the inter-war period a whole arsenal of economic devices for fostering domestic prosperity "at the expense of the foreigner" was thrown into action. As it turned out, these devices seldom succeeded in promoting the economic welfare of the countries imposing them. Without exception, they injured some groups within the country adopting them; and without exception, they prompted retaliatory measures from other countries. The net effect was to reduce the volume of trade, and so of employment. In 1937 industrial production in most countries of importance in international affairs was somewhere around the 1929 level; but the volume of international trade was only one-third of the 1929 level. Restrictionist measures proved a failure for the promotion of internal prosperity. Moreover, they made it possible for the "have-nots" to blame internal difficulties upon the malice of the other nations. Scarcities of foods and raw materials were blamed on the "shortage of foreign exchange" and thus the onus was placed in some vague way upon the foreigner.[5] International economic conflict was a contributing factor — perhaps even a major cause — of World War II. What is the likelihood that current economic conflicts will lead to still a third World War within the life-span of people who remember the first one?

Economic Conflict and the Danger of World War III

On the favourable side of the ledger is the fact that more organized effort is being made to eliminate economic conflict than ever before. The United Nations has associated with it a group of specialized agencies with the primary purpose of reducing the objective bases of international economic conflict. The International Labour Organization pursues this objective by trying to improve social conditions the world over, to reduce the spreads between standards of living in various countries, and to spread throughout the world improved standards of working conditions, health, and security. The International Monetary Fund endeavours to reduce or offset unfavourable balances of payments, making it unnecessary for any country to solve its foreign exchange problems by adopting policies inimical to its internal economic health; it also tries to make chronic creditor countries share with the debtors the responsibility for removing disequilibrium in balances of payments, and to provide a legal framework within which foreign exchange problems can be settled by

5 Cf. Benjamin Higgins, "The Economic War Since 1918", in Willard Waller (ed.), *War in the Twentieth Century*, New York 1940.

international agreement, rather than by economic warfare. The International Bank for Reconstruction and Development makes its contribution (or hopes to do so) by providing capital obtained from prosperous and highly developed countries, to raise productivity in devastated or under-developed countries. The Food and Agriculture Organization seeks to alleviate the economic insecurity of agricultural nations (and of agricultural groups in other nations) arising from extreme fluctuations in demand for agricultural products, and also to provide for a better distribution of the world's food supply, to abolish starvation and malnutrition from the poorer countries. The International Trade Organization is endeavouring to reduce by international agreement the barriers to a free international flow of goods and services.

Taken together, the current activities and future ambitions of these United Nations agencies constitute an integrated programme to reduce, and perhaps ultimately to eliminate, the objective economic causes of international conflict. There is no doubt in my own mind that this programme is the most promising approach to the problem of international economic conflict, and that it will succeed if given the whole-hearted support of all members of the United Nations. The difficulty is, of course, that these agencies have no sovereignty in the member countries; responsibility rests ultimately with the governments of the individual member nations to put into effect the policies that would remove the objective causes of economic conflict.

There is also the possibility mentioned above that even if objective causes are removed, peoples of various countries may *think* that they have a basic grievance against the people of other countries, or against their rulers. UNESCO is currently at work on this sort of problem, especially in its psychological aspects. But economic conditions such as inflation, depression, gross inequalities in income, flagrant wastes of resources, and stagnation, are precisely the conditions in which international as well as internal frictions are most likely to develop. Inflation and unemployment are especially productive of international conflict.

In his foreword to Dr. Bresciani-Turroni's classic study of

the German inflation of 1914-23, Professor Lionel Robbins says that "next probably to the Great War itself, it must bear responsibility for many of the political and economic difficulties of our generation. It destroyed the wealth of the more solid elements in German society: and it left behind a moral and economic disequilibrium, apt breeding ground for the disasters which have followed. Hitler is the foster-child of the inflation."[6] The great depression, and World War II, were in part at least the outcome of the hyper-inflations of the 'twenties. The distortions resulting from inflation weakened the Central and Western European economics, thus intensifying and prolonging the world depression of the 'thirties. By 1933, the German people, who had suffered most were ready to listen to anybody who promised jobs and security — even to Hitler, who led them inevitably towards a disastrous war.

The destruction of the middle classes, impoverishment of the workers, and enrichment of speculators and black marketeers, intensifies social conflict and creates conditions in which radical parties of right or left can take power. In Germany, says Bresciani-Turroni, "Among the old middle classes, ruined by inflation, extreme nationalist propaganda made rapid headway, and among the workers communist ideas spread. The paper inflation, by reinforcing the economic position of those classes which formed the backbone of the 'Right' parties . . . encouraged the political reaction against democracy . . . The funds collected by the big trade unions and by the Socialist party evaporated. The working classes were beaten by the inflation . . . "[7] — and Hitler won.

I have already summarized elsewhere[8] the argument of a leading American economist to the effect that a bad German monetary theory was the cause of World War II, but it is worth repeating. The argument ran as follows: After World War I the economic advisers of the German government, having been trained exclusively in the historical tradition, and

---

6 Constantino Bresciani-Turroni, *The Economics of Inflation*, London 1937, p. 5.
7 *Op. cit.*, pp. 330-332.
8 "The Modern Theory of Economic Fluctuations," in G. Hoover (ed.), *Twentieth Century Economic Thought*, New York 1950, pp. 249-50.

understanding nothing of modern economic analysis, failed to see the simple and obvious relation between monetary expansion, price rises, and depreciation of the reichsmark. They therefore failed to stop the hyper-inflation until the price index rose to 1,260,000,000 (1913 base = 1), rentiers and middle class savers were wiped out, and baskets of money were needed for a day's shopping. The bitter experience of the 1920's made the German people more frightened of inflation than of any other kind of economic disaster, and linked inflation inseparably in their minds with budget deficits and a depreciation of the mark. When the great depression came along, therefore, the Social Democrat government considered it politically impossible to follow other countries in the devaluation of their currency to stimulate exports, and in the use of deficit-financed public expenditures to reduce unemployment. They clung to the gold standard, and struggled valiantly but futilely to balance the budget by raising taxes and cutting expenditures. The result was continually falling incomes and rising unemployment. Eventually the Germans, most of whom could remember nothing more pleasant than war, inflation, and depression, were ready to listen to Hitler. Once in power, Hitler abandoned "orthodox" finance and quickly restored full employment, a fact which helped to consolidate his hold on the German people. The stage for World War II was set.

The author of this argument would of course admit that it is a grossly over-simplified account of the events leading up to World War II, but he would insist that it has a large element of truth in it, and I would agree. Inflation and depression are among the major factors that can lead to social conflict, revolution, or war.

If this argument is correct, the maintenance of peace and the maintenance of prosperity are very closely related. If full employment without inflation is quickly achieved and maintained forever more, the chances of parties of the extreme right or left coming to power in the western democracies is rather small. If the objectives of an optimum income distribution, an optimum allocation of resources, and an optimum rate of economic progress are achieved as well, the chances of revolutions — bloodless or gory — are even smaller. And if the western democracies avoid the internal threats from both the extreme right and the extreme left, it is unlikely that they will find it either necessary or desirable to wage war, at least on economic grounds. I have yet to be provided with convincing evidence that Russia has extensive territorial ambitions, *apart from* the insecurity she naturally feels in a hostile world. The area already under Russian control is enormously rich in natural resources; the Russian standard of living is still low. For the next few decades, Russia will have her hands full raising the standard of living of her own millions by developing her own resources. If Russia were assured of the safety of her economic and social system from both internal and external aggression, I doubt whether she would be much interested in extending her borders.

The same is true of the United States. The American people are not "imperialistic" in the usual sense of the term; they have little interest in building up an "American empire". But they are very jealous of their economic and social system, and are prepared to fight to defend it. So long as their system functions well, there will be no serious threat from within; but if it breaks down, the chances are very strong that the internal threat from the left will become more significant. Such a development could lead to consolidation of the forces on the right, a broadening of the term "Communist" to include all critics of the Big Business version of American "individualism" (which, as pointed out in an earlier lecture, is really insistence on "the freedom to exploit", or freedom to buy cheap and sell dear), and the emergence of an American form of fascism. An economically successful and progressive American democracy can, I believe, live peacefully in the same world with an economically successful and progressive Russian socialism. I do not believe that a fascist America can live peacefully with any kind of Russian socialism, especially if the latter is expansionist through fear of aggression.

I am not prepared to argue that neither the U.S.A. nor the U.S.S.R. could conceivably become aggressive unless their economic systems fail dramatically, or threatened to do so. There are people who insist that the fighting which broke out in Korea in May 1950 was the result of Russian aggression, and others who maintain that the United States was the true aggressor. But I do contend that there would be no *economic* basis for conflict between them, if each pursued, within its own economic framework, the objectives laid down in the third lecture of this series. And, as was also indicated in that lecture, there is no *economic* reason why both systems should not succeed. We need only the will.

Moreover, the measures necessary to achieve these objectives within single countries would do much to eliminate the kind of economic warfare that raged from 1918 to 1939. Full employment without inflation does not require restrictions on foreign trade; and an optimum allocation of resources, even in a single country, requires that over the long run trade in goods and services be balanced at a high level, and also that nothing should be produced at home that could be imported more cheaply. The use of tariffs, quotas, and exchange control to restrict the free flow of goods and services is quite inconsistent with the pursuit of an optimum allocation of resources. An optimal rate of economic growth, as well as an optimal distribution of resources, requires each under-populated country to seek an optimum population; and if every under-populated country took only enough immigrants to raise its *own* populations to the level that would maximize *per capita* output, over-population elsewhere would be significantly relieved.

General Conclusions

These, then, are my conclusions regarding the economic causes of social conflict, revolution, and war in the present historical context. First, the threat of World War III arises more out of the clash of two rival economic ideologies than it does out of the clash of two rival world powers; would anyone deny that the danger of war would be very much less if the U.S.A. were communist, or if the U.S.S.R. were a democracy of the western capitalist variety? Second, the clash between these two economic and social systems would be much less serious if neither system were threatened from within. The best way to preserve western democracy is to make it function efficiently in the economic sphere. Communism cannot be killed by defeating Russia; and if the western world can find a way to maintain a smooth-working economy within a democratic political framework, it need have little fear of aggression, at least from within. In the last two lectures of this series, I shall argue that the only serious obstacle to the achievement of this objective is the failure of individuals, and the powerful groups into which they are organized, to recognize their moral responsibility to society, and to abandon their selfish individual or group economic interests in favour of those of society as a whole.

V

ECONOMIC POLICY AND THE "BIG THREE"

IN MY FIRST TWO LECTURES I concluded that the extent of
knowledge and of agreement among economists was sufficient
to permit them to make policy recommendations on which
the bulk of economists could agree, if the objectives were
clearly stated. In the third lecture, I outlined a set of objectives of policy which seem to me to be unambiguous and
non-controversial, provided certain basic value judgments are
accepted. In the fourth lecture I intimated that economic
conflicts arise mainly from the exercise by the Big Three
(Big Business, Big Labour, and Big Agriculture) of their
"freedom to exploit"; that is, the freedom to use their bargaining power to the full, in order to enhance their level of
real income, or the prestige they derive from *control* of the
production and distribution of goods and services. I pointed
out that the objective economic bases of international conflict are, to a large extent, the same as the objective economic
causes of internal economic conflict.

Political conflicts reflect these economic conflicts. In Australia, the Big Three are roughly represented by three distinct political parties. In the United States of America and
in the United Kingdom there are only two major parties, but
political events depend a great deal on how much pressure
can be brought to bear by each of the three major lobbying
groups on *whichever* of the two major parties is in power.
This state of affairs is particularly noticeable in the United
States of America, where the economic and political position
of the two major parties is not markedly dissimilar. What
counts in the politics of that country is not so much which
party gets elected to Congress, but how much power can be
mobilized by business, labour, and agriculture to bring pressure on whichever party happens to be elected. In Canada,
the situation is rather more complex. There are two major
political parties, plus a socialist party deriving its most solid
support from the embattled farmer. But the three major
pressure groups are the same nevertheless, and the outcome

of parliamentary debates depends a good deal on the lobbying power of these three major economic groups.

One of the reasons for the marked success of war-time economic policy in Australia, Canada, the United Kingdom and the United States of America, was the co-operation of business men, farmers and workers with professional economists and with governments. War-time economic policy in these countries was largely formulated by professional economists, in consultation with governments and the Big Three, and it was administered by business men, farmers, workers, and government officials, in consultation with professional economists. This same sort of team work must become a permanent feature of democratic society if economic policy is to be equally successful in meeting the problems of peace. The general nature of these problems and of the policies needed to deal with them are quite clear; but the adoption and administration of the necessary policies require the support of business, of labour and of agriculture.

At the present time, there seems to be more danger of a rift between economists and business than between economists and either of the other two groups. Also, business was the first of the three groups to become "big". I shall therefore begin by outlining the nature of the economic problems facing business, the consequent attitude of business towards economic policy, and the expressed reason for business mistrust of economics. I shall also state briefly some reasons why economists, in turn, have misgivings regarding business. I shall then go through the same procedure for Big Labour and Big Agriculture.

Economic Policy and Big Business

Business Problems

The major problem of business, I believe, is the inherent tendency for profits to fall in a capitalist system. This tendency results partly from diminishing returns to land and partly from a natural tendency for returns to capital to diminish. The tendency of profits to fall is a crucial part of the Classical theory of economic development, of the Marxist theory, and of the Schumpeter theory. Indeed, I know of no theory of economic development, or of any set of historical facts, which would indicate anything other than an inherent tendency for profits to fall. This tendency can be offset either by a sufficient rate of technological progress or by a sufficient rate of increase in monopoly power. Consequently, business activity has been directed partly towards discovering new techniques, new commodities, and new resources, and partly towards trying to consolidate monopoly positions or to create new ones.

Of course, it is possible for the rate of profit, in the sense of the percentage rate of return on investment, to fall without the share of profits in national income falling. If the growth in the total stock of capital is rapid enough to offset the decline in the rate of return per million pounds' worth of investment, then the total share of capital in the national income can be maintained. Such statistics as are available indicate no clear trend towards a decline in profits (including dividends, interest, rents and entrepreneurial withdrawals) as a proportion of the national income. But this failure of profits to fall as a share of national income is, in part, a reflection of the success of business in maintaining a rapid rate of technological progress and a rapid rate of capital accumulation on the one hand, and the success in establishing more and more firmly entrenched monopoly positions on the other.

A second major business problem is the instability of profits. The percentage fluctuations of profit in the course of the business cycle are considerably greater than the percentage fluctuations in wages. This problem causes capitalists (using the term "capitalists" to mean all those who derive their income in the form of "profits" as defined above), considerable concern.

A third problem faced by the profit-earning group is the difficulty of maintaining its status and prestige within the capitalist framework. Professor Schumpeter argues that Capitalism, by its very success, creates a social and political environment hostile to capitalist development — a social climate antipathetic to the "New Men" who create New Firms, set up New Plant and Equipment, and thus engender economic expansion. A good example of this sort of development was the hostility to big business demonstrated by the American New Deal. Schumpeter points to such New Deal measures as undistributed profits taxes, capital gains taxes, social security taxes, public housing legislation, labour legislation, and public investment programmes, which changed the rules of the business game, and shifted responsibility for economic decisions from business men to government officials. Such matters worry the business man at least as much as the tendency for profits to fall in the absence of offsetting factors.

One experience brought this fact home to me in striking fashion. Early in the war, a government agency to which I was attached had a conference at the Edgewater Beach Hotel in Chicago, an expensive and elegant hotel with a good many permanent residents.[1] The hotel, being rather far out from town, maintains a limousine to take its permanent residents to the shopping centre. The limousine has "Edgewater Beach Hotel" in discreet letters on the panel of the door. One morning, riding into town in this limousine, I sat behind two mink-coated, diamond-bedecked dowagers who were talking about "that man in the White House" and "that rabble-rouser — Roosevelt" and the evil days of the mid-1930's. One of them said: "Do you know, in 1934 and 1935, when I used to ride into town in the hotel limousine, people used to *throw stones* at us!" That was the kind of thing about the New Deal that hurt the business and financial community most. Such people had become used to having others say that since they lived at the Edgewater Hotel, they must be very rich, and therefore very great and very good. In the 1920's, this attitude was common enough in America. If a man was rich and successful, he was by definition also good and kind and great and wise, and indeed a repository of all the virtues. The depression and the New Deal together destroyed this attitude. Business men and bankers blamed their loss of prestige on Roosevelt, and hated him for it.

It is apparent that if the position of the capitalist is

---

[1] And which, it should be made clear, civil servants could ill afford on their *per diem* travel allowances!

undermined by the very success of capitalism — as Schumpeter insists — it is also undermined by the failures of
capitalism. The spectacular collapse of the existing order
in the 1930's destroyed the faith of millions of people in the
economic and social system and in its leaders. The business
man is thus in a very awkward position. His success leads to
hostility, and the failure of the system of which he is the
leader also leads to hostility. No wonder he has some sleepless
nights!

Business Attitude Towards Economic Policy

The business man usually believes that what is good for
business is good for society. He finds some support for this
view in the economics of the past. Adam Smith refers to the
"invisible hand" which guides us in pursuit of our selfish
interests to further the ends of society as a whole. Adam
Smith was actually more of an interventionist than the
business community would care to recollect; but it is the
laissez-faire statements by Adam Smith that seem to have
survived. One finds a clearer expression of the business view
in the writings of J. B. Clark, who argued that a freely
working economy would necessarily produce the optimal
situation from a social point of view. In the late nineteenth
century, American Chairs of Economics were frequently
occupied by theologians, who tended to argue that the free
enterprise system was divine. Many business men, particularly in the United States, have been brought up on that
kind of economics.

Because of his belief that what is good for business is good
for society, the business man tends to identify the "practical"
and the "real" with the profitable. Indeed, the business man
uses the term "impracticable" or "unreal" as a synonym for
"unprofitable". Australian business men have said recently,
"The 40-hour week is unreal; it is impracticable." Well, the
40-hour week is very real. But it was considered to be unprofitable and therefore, by definition, it was "impracticable"
and "unreal".

Because of his interest in maintaining the prestige and
status of the business man as the controller of society, if he

feels that the government has to do something about the economic situation, the business man prefers policies which are automatic in their operation, and which require no day-to-day decisions by government officials. If something *has* to be done, he prefers a new law to a new government agency; for if only a new law is involved, the legislature acts and thereafter leaves the economy free again, with no control exerted by government bureaucrats, and therefore no transfer of prestige from the business man to the government official.

Finally, despite the professed belief in *laissez-faire*, the business man is typically opposed to free trade. He is a protectionist, and as such contributes to the causes of international conflict. It is interesting to see that the business man has dropped the one aspect of *laissez-faire* to which Adam Smith gave virtually unqualified support — international free trade.

Why Business Distrusts Economists

The attitude of business towards economics and economists is derived from these views on economic policy. There seem to be four major reasons why business distrusts economics. First, economists are regarded as impractical, long-haired theorists. Second, it is argued that economics is not a science. Third, it is felt that all economists are radicals. Fourth, economists are considered incompetent because they earn less than business men. Let us consider these points, one by one.

It is true, of course, that most economists have never met a payroll. It is also true that business experience can be a useful supplement to the economist's training, as is evidenced by the contribution to the content of economic knowledge made by business men who have studied the subject carefully. However, the work of economists with business experience is not clearly distinguishable from the work of other economists. Indeed, some of the most highly theoretical work has been done by "practical" men. Witness, for example, the writings of Vilfredo Pareto, a successful engineer before becoming Professor of Economics at Lausanne and writing very abstract economics, or of H. G. Littler, General Manager of the Chemical Division of Canadian Industries Ltd. — the Canadian component of the great international chemicals cartel — who writes a very pure form of mathematical monetary theory, or of Fritz Machlup and William Fellner in the United States. Moreover, a knowledge of business itself is, in no sense, a knowledge of economics. To argue that business experience provides the basis for determining economic policy is like arguing that anyone who has ever used a riveting machine can run a steel mill. A surgeon who has had appendicitis may possibly perform a more perfect appendectonomy than one who has not; but most people would rather have their appendix removed by a surgeon who has never had appendicitis than by someone who has had appendicitis but who has no medical training. In the same way, a detailed knowledge of the problems and administration of a particular business is not equivalent to understanding of the economic system as a whole, and only the specialized training of the economist is really adequate for dealing with general economic problems.

The business man usually does not understand the method of the economist, nor indeed scientific method of any kind; but he knows that economists do not understand his business as well as he does, and he concludes that the economist does not know much about other businesses either; therefore, he reasons, the economist knows nothing about business as a whole, and consequently the economist knows nothing about the economy.

It is true, of course, that the study of economics may lead to no immediate increase in business profits. It is also true that the recommendations of economists sometimes reduce profits. However, contrary to business opinion, "practical" and "profitable" are *not* synonymous. Policies designed to restrict output and raise prices may be "practical" for the business man in the short run; they are quite "impractical" for the consumer, and may prove impractical for business in the long run if the ire of the consuming public is sufficiently aroused. Similarly, a policy of resisting wage increases may be "practical" for business in the short run, but it is impractical from the workers' point of view, and may also prove impractical for business if insufficient purchasing power is available to provide markets for its products, or if it leads to a general strike. Some policies are practical even if painful for business; and there is surely nothing practical about loose or wishful thinking, or short-sighted selfishness or ostrich tactics.

Some business men object to the use of abstraction in economic analysis. However, as I pointed out in an earlier lecture, abstraction is essential to scientific analysis of any kind. The sin of the economist is not that he makes abstractions, but that he sometimes fails to resist the temptation to make policy recommendations on the basis of models that are still abstract. He tends to design his bomb sight on the basis of the law of gravity alone. However, in economics, nothing is "all right in theory" that "will not work out in practice". If it will not work, a theory is either incorrect or incomplete.

A closely related view of the business man is that since economics is not a science, it is merely a matter of opinion, and the opinion of one man is about as good as that of another. I do not insist that economics is a science, since the question is largely one of definition; but I do insist that economics is scientific. The methodology of economics is much the same as in other fields universally accepted as sciences; and economic analysis is kept as free from value judgments as possible. The business man's failure to understand this fact is, I think, one of the major reasons for lack of sympathy between business and economics. Economics is not a matter of opinion, but a matter of rigorous analysis. Economics is, perhaps, more a matter of opinion than is physics, in the sense that there are more factors operating that are not subject to physical control. On the other hand, it is probably somewhat less a matter of opinion than is medicine. What is essential in economics, as in medicine, is that the scientific *basis* of conclusions reached should be recognized and respected. If people said to their doctors,

"You say I have appendicitis — that is just your opinion. It is my opinion that I have constipation — and I shall accordingly take a laxative", there would be more deaths from appendicitis. Perhaps the high mortality rates of business firms is partly the result of treating economics as "just a matter of opinion!"

There is a striking similarity between the business man's epistemology and the Marxist epistemology. The Marxist and the business man have the same ideas about the nature of truth in the field of economics. Both deny the usefulness of abstracting economics from its political context. Both argue that attitudes towards economic policies depend mainly on who butters the economist's bread. Thus, the Marxist argues that most economists in capitalist countries are apologists for the capitalist system because they are hired either by academic institutions or by governments, and that both academic institutions and governments are merely creatures of the ruling capitalist class. The business man, in similar vein, despite converse conclusions, argues that because most economists work mainly for universities or for government departments, they have acquired an anti-business bias. Thus, in a recent publication of the United States Chamber of Commerce, Emerson P. Schmidt, Director of Research for the United States Chamber of Commerce, says:

In the first place we must remind ourselves that "professionally trained economists as we know them now" are practitioners of a speciality for which there have been only two important "markets": the academic and the governmental. May this not have over-stimulated "governmental" solutions to our problems, with a consequent slighting of the possible contributions through the action of individual business firms? As business organizations, including chambers of commerce and trade associations, become a more and more important third market, the term "professionally trained economist" can hardly be expected to go on having just the same meaning. With a larger and larger section of the profession acquiring the new type of experience in the new type of assignment, the whole profession cannot but reflect the change. Training in economics will itself undergo more or less predictable changes. For one thing, in economics, as well as any other field, the kind of textbooks that are written will inevitably change with any major development affecting the interests and experience of "the professionals" concerned. In the second place, when there is an important business-world market for economic analysts, neither teaching nor learning could hardly be expected to be the same as when the only important markets were academic and governmental.

The belief that all economists are radicals is closely associated with the belief that economics is not scientific. Indeed, once it is admitted that economics is a matter of analysis and not a matter of opinion, it becomes obvious that economics could not be radical in itself, any more than medicine could be radical in itself. There are a few competent economists who are communists, some who are socialists, many who are liberals, some who are conservative, and a very few who are fascist. Yet, these differences in political views have surprisingly little effect upon the economic analysis of the people concerned. It is instructive to compare two books on the theory of wages — one written by a Marxist, Maurice Dobb and one by an economist who was at the time a leading anti-socialist, Lionel Robbins. There is strikingly little difference in the analysis of the process of wage determination in the two books. When an economist becomes a party-line communist or a dyed-in-the-wool conservative, other considerations than those pertaining to pure economic analysis are always involved.

The final argument presented by the business man to prove the untrustworthiness of the economist is his relative poverty. It is true that in Australia, and the United Kingdom, few economists in government or academic life earn more than £2,000 a year. In Canada, few economists earn more than $8,000 per year, and even in the United States there are not many who earn more than $15,000 a year. Why should any one with any brains accept such a paltry sum when he can earn so much more in business life?

I think the answer to this question is apparent from its phrasing. I could mention several men whose incomes are relatively low compared with men similarly placed in business life and who did extremely useful and intelligent work in recent years. Their names are Eisenhower, Patton, Montgomery, MacArthur, and the others. Surely it cannot be said that all Prime Ministers are necessarily stupid because they accept a job paying only £3,000 a year! And what of the captains of industry who moved to Canberra, London, Ottawa and Washington during the war at salaries ranging from $1·00 to $10,000 a year? Were they *all* men who suddenly lost their business ability?

Of course, this action on the part of business men was the result of war-time patriotism. But this is precisely the point. The patriotism of the governmental or academic economist is not limited to war periods. He knows that national emergencies are always imminent and the ideal of public service continues to guide him in peace as in war. Those academic economists who have chosen to do so have demonstrated their practicality and ability to earn high incomes in no uncertain terms. I think, for example, of Leon Henderson, former administrator of the O.P.A. — one of the most hated men in the United States of America — who, after being forced out of his government job by business pressure on Congress, went into the business sphere and earned a reputed $100,000 a year. Yet, I am sure that Henderson would have preferred to stay at his $10,000 post in the government had he been able to do so. Indeed, he later returned to the government service when the political situation made it possible. I think, also, of Beardsley Ruml, a former college professor, who is now Treasurer of R. H. Macy and Co., the biggest department store in the world, and Chairman of the Federal Reserve Board in New York, and who is said to have saved his company his high salary many times over in his savings to Macy and Co. through suggestions for reorganization. The most obvious case is that of Lord Keynes himself who, as treasurer of King's College, Cambridge, proved so astute an investor of funds that mere rumours of his operations caused fluctuations on the London Stock Exchange. Indeed, Keynes was probably one of the most successful financiers of his generation. He is said to have quadrupled the King's College endowment in a few years, earning an average of 20 per cent on his investments. Certainly he accumulated a large personal fortune.[2]

Nearly all economists face — often several times in their career — a choice between higher income and a higher degree of public service. Surely, it is not to their discredit that they so often choose the latter.

Why Economists Distrust Business Men

The basis of economists' misgivings concerning business men is implied in what I have already said. It consists of a feeling that the business man makes his decisions in terms of advantage to his firm rather than in terms of social welfare; that he lacks an objective and scientific approach to economic affairs, and that consequently he too easily identifies the welfare of the economy as a whole with his own profits. Indeed, even so progressive a business man as Eric Johnston recently told a group of business economists that "a business economist, of course, has an overwhelming responsibility to his employer; the economist must serve his employer's interest". Economists feel — perhaps wrongly — that few business men deliberately sacrifice profit in order to improve the lot of the consumer or of the worker. Even in Australia some business men think that an occasional depression is a good thing because it makes it possible to force down wages. So long as such attitudes are expressed by business men, the economist, who is interested in maximizing the standard of living of society as a whole, will naturally feel that control of economic life cannot be safely left to business men alone.

The second reason for lack of confidence in the business man is his tendency to substitute opinions and wishful thinking for objective analysis. So prevalent is the polemical or argumentative approach among business men that they

---

[2] An appreciative business colleague wrote shortly after Keynes' death, "In the numerous tributes which have already appeared full justice has been done to Keynes' manifold public services, while his wonderful academic career has also been extolled, but I have not noticed any testimony from the city where he had for a long period many important interests. As manager of the Life Assurance Society of which he was Chairman for nineteen years, I enjoyed special opportunities for close contact both officially and socially. And what an inspiration he was for men of lesser breed. Under his influence, investment theory and practice were revolutionized; and investment in ordinary shares was one of his special contributions to life assurance theory.

are inclined to impute the same kind of tactics to others, including economists. The business man seems inclined to think that "economists favour public housing because they are all socialists" and that, since he is not a socialist, he should therefore oppose public housing. I have even been told by a prominent mining engineer that, in his opinion, the *best* analyses are those that *start* by taking a position and then supporting it. This attitude is so directly contradictory to the scientific approach that the conclusions of business men are naturally suspected by economists.

Finally, the economist knows, and fears that the business man does not know, that a clash between the interests of individual firms and the interests of society as a whole arises whenever a firm is big enough or strong enough to exercise any control over the prices it pays and the prices it gets. Under such conditions, the maximum profit level of output will be lower than the maximum satisfaction level, and any firm that limits its output to the maximum profit level is contributing to misallocation of resources.

There are even clashes of interest between one business and business as a whole. For example, if depression threatens, it is good policy for a single firm to dispose of excess inventories and build up its cash balances; but if all firms adopt this policy depression is assured. It pays one firm to pay low wages, but if all firms pay low wages they will have to accept low prices, since the purchasing power to support a high price structure will not be in the hands of the people who comprise the bulk of the market. In a period of inflation, it may pay a single firm to avoid taxes, but if all firms avoid taxes, and spend the money instead, inflation will be aggravated. In a down-swing, it is good policy for one firm to save money and build up reserves, but if all firms attempt to save they will all fail, because the attempt to save rather than spend will reduce national income further, and so reduce the profits that provide the funds to be saved. And so on.

Highly unorthodox it was then, as were many other principles he from time to time advocated, but long since commonplace and now respectable. . . . To have rubbed shoulders with this man of genius leaves behind a rich and rare fragrance which will remain always to those who have experienced it" (Letter in *The Economist*, 11 May 1946).

There are other, more subtle, clashes between the short-run interests of all business and the long-run interests. For example, at a certain stage of an up-swing an increase in the share of national income going to profits will produce a rate of increase in profits that cannot be maintained, since insufficient income is being distributed to those who comprise the market; investment decisions based on that rate of increase in profits are foredoomed to failure, and the reaction to the disappointment may launch a general down-swing in which profits will be wiped out altogether. Economists feel that business men cannot be entrusted with any large measure of control over economic policy until they show very clearly that they have learned the difference between their short-run and their long-run interests, between the interest of one firm and the interest of all firms, and between the interest of business as a whole and the interest of society as a whole.

Economic Policy and Big Labour

Problems of Labour

The fundamental problem of the worker is still poverty. In a 40-hour week the average Australian male worker, who is one of the best paid workers in the world, was earning less than £8 10s. per week, even at the end of 1949. The average British male worker was earning just over £6, the average Canadian male worker $40, in a 40-hour week. Even in the United States the average wage for a man working a 40-hour week was only $56[3]. With the inflated price levels prevailing at that time, these amounts were far from riches. Worse still, the position of the worker is such that it is extremely difficult for him to improve his economic situation. The continuous pressure on his family budget makes it extremely hard for him to save. The working class in this country, in the United States of America, in Canada and in the United Kingdom, saves virtually nothing as a group. The savings of workers in the higher wage brackets are largely offset by the excess of spending over earnings by workers in the lower wage

---

[3] *International Labour Review,* May 1950, pp. 559-64.

brackets. That was true even in 1947, with full employment and a higher level of wages that had been achieved.

Moreover, labour has experienced great difficulty in improving its relative position in capitalist societies. Labour's share of national income has been remarkably constant in recent decades. Even the growth of powerful trade unions seems to have had no clear-cut effect on the share of the workers in national income. In the case of Australia, reliable figures are available only for 1928-1929 and from 1938-1939 to date. These figures reveal that in 1928-1929 workers obtained 58.6 per cent of the national income. In 1938-1939 they got 59.4 per cent of the national income. In the middle of the war period they received 66·7 per cent.[4] In 1947-1948 they got 56.7 per cent of the national income — slightly below the 1928-1929 figure. Thus, over the 20-year period, there is no evidence of a rise in labour's share of national income before taxes. Figures for manufacturing alone show that the share of wages and salaries in the total manufacturing income averaged between 52 per cent and 54 per cent for the years 1900-1939. The same stability of labour's share has appeared in Canada, the United Kingdom and the United States of America. New Zealand shows a remarkable stability of labour's share up to 1936, a substantial increase during the war years, and a slight decline since. The main conclusion is that the growth of trade unionism has been barely able to maintain labour's share of the national income, in the face of increasingly powerful employer organizations. There is no convincing evidence that trade unionism has succeeded in substantially raising labour's share.

What is worse, the workers, whose share of the national income is low relative to their numbers, do the more unpleasant, uninteresting and unhealthy jobs. Finally, the social status of the worker is still relatively low.

When considering the current labour situation, it is important to remember the long history of ruthless exploitation of the worker. Mantoux, in his book on the industrial revolution, tells some pretty tales, such as the story of employers who hung child employees over operating machines

---

4 This figure includes pay and allowances of the Armed Forces.

by their wrists, so that the miserable children had to keep their knees bent up to avoid having their feet cut off, if they showed any sign of slackening their efforts during their 13 or 14 hours working day.[5] One tends to forget past atrocities in the face of the marked improvement of labour's bargaining power and standard of living in recent generations; but the tendency for labour to use its bargaining power to the full springs from maltreatment in the past.

The worker also suffers from insecurity, associated with the contingencies of accident, disease, death, and unemployment. It is true that this insecurity has been alleviated in recent decades, by unemployment insurance, accident insurance, death benefits and the like. But labour has had to fight for those gains; they did not come as a gift.

Labour's Attitude Towards Economic Policy

The attitude of the worker towards policy clearly arises out of these problems. The worker feels that policy must guarantee him full employment and social security. Even today, the threat of unemployment makes him afraid of technological progress. In Sydney recently I read a newspaper account of the pressure brought to bear on the Trades Hall authorities to employ a liftman, because the coal strike was causing unemployment. There is an automatic lift at the Trades Hall in Sydney, which meant that "one man is kept out of a job". This situation was considered criminal during a period of unemployment. The employment of a liftman would not only "give one man a job", it would also "improve the service", because Trades Hall visitors were deliberately leaving the lift doors open, to make it *necessary* to employ a liftman!

The fear of unemployment also results in the "ca' canny" tactics prevalent in the building industry, the reluctance to work at full speed for fear that the store of jobs will be exhausted. The fear of unemployment also appears in opposition to any increase in stocks. Any increase in inventories

---

5 Paul Mantoux, *The Industrial Revolution in the Eighteenth Century* (New York, 1927), p. 424.

is considered a threat to future employment, and so leads to absenteeism and "regulatory" strikes.

The worker also feels that policy should be so designed as to increase his share in the national income. This goal is extremely difficult to obtain in a capitalist society. Within the market system, it is virtually impossible to raise labour's share of the national income without price control. This fact is illustrated by war-time experience. While price control operated in Australia, Canada, the United States of America and the United Kingdom, labour's share of the national income did increase.[6] As price controls were relaxed after the war, labour's share of the national income dropped towards pre-war figures.

The difficulty of raising labour's share by market tactics leads to a growing emphasis by organized labour on redistributing income through "fiscal policy", that is, through taxes and government spending. Social security programmes financed by taxes on the upper income groups have been particularly popular with labour. But redistributing income by fiscal policy also encounters difficulties. In the United States of America, for example, the distribution of national income scarcely changed between 1941 and 1948, despite the enormous increase in income tax and the growth of social security programmes. What has happened since the United States entered the war in 1941 is that the top fifth of the income scale has lost 4.5 per cent of the national income; the lowest fifth has gained six-tenths of one per cent of the national income; the next lowest fifth has gained one and a half per cent; the middle fifth gained one per cent; and the next fifth gained 1.4 per cent of the national income. The significance of this redistribution is substantial to those in the top fifth who have lost it, but it is practically nil to those who have gained the increases.

Even in the United Kingdom, where the income tax has been kept at a much higher level, and where the scale of social security outlays is bigger, the proportion of national

---

6 Assuming that the proportion of workers to others in the Armed Forces was no lower than in the economy as a whole.

income going into wages and salaries *after income tax* was only nine per cent higher in 1948 than it was before the war. Now, again, that nine per cent of the national income taken from the few in the upper income groups, is very significant; but spread among the many in the lower income groups, it does not mean very much to individual families. Yet before the war, the British fiscal system scarcely redistributed income at all; only the bottom ten per cent of the income scale were net gainers from the fiscal process, and other income groups lost by it. Consequently, the upper income groups are disgruntled and the lower income groups are dissatisfied. Political friction with respect to income distribution, if not actually intensified, has certainly not been removed, by recent egalitarian policies. It is certainly easier to redistribute income through the fiscal process than through the market. But even with the direct intervention of government, group conflict with respect to distribution of national income is very hard to eliminate.[7]

Finally, the worker, no less than the business man, tends to be protectionist. He fears the effect of international competition on his standard of living — particularly the competition of so-called "low-wage-standard countries" — and, by the same token, he tends to oppose immigration. The business man is often in the position of favouring immigration, because he hopes to get labour at a cheaper rate, and to provide a market for his supplies; but the worker is typically hostile to free immigration. In this way, the worker, no less than the business man, contributes to international conflict.

Labour's Attitude Towards Economists

Labour's attitude towards economists is less articulate than the business attitude. It overlaps the attitude of the Marxists, discussed previously (p. 119). Even among workers who are not communists (and most of them in the western world

---

[7] In the United Kingdom, the problem is further aggravated by the fact that any equalization of income adds to the difficulty of balancing international accounts, by increasing the demand for imported foodstuffs and raw materials. The devaluation of the pound in 1949 was a means of countermanding such redistribution of real income as had taken place.

are not), there is a tendency to consider the economist an apologist for the *status quo* unless he has been clearly labelled as a "labour economist" or as a "socialist economist". In so far as he thinks of economists as a breed at all, the worker is no less anxious than the business man to pin a label on economists, to distinguish the "conservative" from the "socialist" and so on. Like the business man, too, the worker feels that the economist is "unreal", but for somewhat different reasons. The economist, sheltered in his ivory towers, does not face the hard facts of life; consequently, the economist cannot have any real heart-felt sympathy for the worker.

The Economist's Attitude Towards Labour

Actually, most economists have been sympathetic to the under-dog. One would not choose economics as a profession unless one had some concern for social welfare — and that means concern for the welfare of the oppressed members of society. True, economists have sometimes been exponents of a very dismal science. Not so very long ago many economists argued that it was necessary to cut wages during depressions. But it cannot be said that those economists were anti-Labour. Many of the Australian economists who pressed for wage cuts in 1931-1932 were strongly pro-labour, and they have continued to be so. They believed that those wage cuts were necessary for the welfare of the workers as well as for the remainder of society. Moreover, most economists accept labour's objectives. They agree that labour's share of national income should be raised if possible, that full employment should be maintained, and that social security should be extended.

The economist does have some quarrels with organized labour. The economist is well aware that continued improvement in the standard of living of the worker ultimately requires higher productivity. He is opposed to "ca' canny" methods; he is opposed to limitations on the number of bricks laid per hour, to the limitations on the use of labour-saving devices, and so on, because he knows that in the long run *only* labour-saving devices, speedy bricklaying, and the like, will raise labour's standard of living.

The economist is also concerned about the immobility of labour — the reluctance of the workers to move from one occupation to another and from one region to another in response to changes in demand, cost, and technique. He feels, too, that labour misunderstands the nature and size of profits. The tendency of the worker to stress redistribution of income, rather than raising the general level of income, creates many awkward problems. The worker tends to think that an enormous pile of profits is there for the taking, if only he gets his own political representatives into power. But when he gets his representatives into power, he finds that the enormous pile of profits is just not there, as he is currently learning to his sorrow in the United Kingdom. It is true that people who derive their income from profits have high incomes relative to those who derive them from wages, but there are not many of those people; when you calculate what this pile of profits means when distributed among all the workers, you find that it does not amount to very much.

Moreover, there are certain aspects of profits which must exist in any kind of society. Even a Communist society must take account of depreciation on plant and machinery, and make provision for its replacement and for net expansion. It must also pay for management. And even Russia finds it convenient to pay interest for savings.

Economic Policy and Big Agriculture

Big Agriculture is a relative newcomer to the political arena, but is rapidly becoming a major power in democratic countries.

The chief problem of agriculture is the extreme instability of its income. In the United States of America, the index of farm incomes increased from 102 in 1915 to 200 in 1920, and in 1922 it dropped to 102 again. By 1929 it had risen to 160, but it dropped to 63 in 1932, and then rose to 140 in 1937. It was much lower again in 1938. These figures indicate the violent cyclical fluctuations in farm incomes. Other countries have had the same sort of experience. The farmer also has to deal with seasonal fluctuations, which present him with budgeting problems, and with the spasmodic fluctuations arising from vagaries of the climate.

Because of his peculiar competitive position, the farmer finds that his income varies widely, even though his output is relatively stable. Agricultural output actually increased during the early years of the great depression, as the farmer tried to offset falling prices by increasing his acreage and output. The index of output for persons gainfully employed in the United States of America on farms increased from 130 in 1915 to 138 in 1920; but their incomes increased from 102 to 200 in the same period, because prices rose from 100 to 216. In the depths of the depression (1932), output was still 141, prices dropped to 70, and income fell to 63.

In particular fields of agriculture, even more violent fluctuations appear. The income from grain in the United States fell from an average of $1,463 in 1925-1929 to $332 in 1932. Much the same sort of thing happened to incomes from cotton, hogs, cattle and sheep.

Because of the catastrophic drop of farm incomes in depression, the farmer faces a low average level of income over a long period of time. For the farmer it may be a matter of feast or famine, but it is more often famine than feast. During the early 1920's, wheat farmers in the Canadian province of Saskatchewan had *negative* incomes, after the cost of replacing plant and equipment was taken into account. They burned wheat for fuel, because it did not pay them to ship grain to the market; the cost of freight and storage exceeded the price which they could get for their grain. When the second world war began, nearly one-third of the families in Saskatchewan were still on relief.

Furthermore, the farmer faces the problem of intrinsically low bargaining power, because he is in an inherently competitive field. Farming is an industry in which relatively small firms can be efficient. Markets are very wide; very often, they are world markets. Selling organizations of farmers — co-operatives, for example — can be effective only if the market is limited geographically, as it is in the case of milk, or, if there is very little competition, as in the case of

Brazilian coffee, or if the organization is world-wide, as in the case of the rubber cartel. It is more difficult to organize farmers than workers or employers because there is a less obvious community of interest amongst them, and less political solidarity. Agriculture comprises both labour and capital, and the wide range of incomes within the agricultural field tends to split farmers politically. The problem of sheer space — the difficulty of assembling large numbers of farmers in one place — adds to the complexities of effective agricultural organization. The farmer, also, tends to be more exclusively concerned with his own particular products. He thinks in terms of prices for cotton, or wheat, or tobacco, or wool, rather than of the general level of farm prices. The worker tends to be interested in the general level of wages, because he has learned that his own position will almost certainly improve if the general level of wages rises.

Finally, the farmer faces the problem of immobility. Land cannot move. Capital moves very easily so long as it is free and uninvested; even if capital is fixed in plant and equipment, it can be moved in time because the owners need not replace plant and equipment of a particular kind, but can reinvest their returns in something else. Labour can move as freely as it likes — which is sometimes not very freely. But land cannot move at all. True, the owner can transfer land from one use to another, but sometimes the range of possible uses is very narrow, as tends to be the case with wheat, tobacco and citrus fruit land. Moreover, the change from one use to another may take a very long time. Grass land can be converted to wheat quickly enough, but to change wheat land back to grass takes years. Also, there is truth in the old saw that farming is "a way of life"; abandoning your farm means leaving your home as well as your business. This immobility of agriculture increases the dependence of agriculture on exports. Once an agricultural export business has been built up, the development of restrictionism abroad is extremely serious. Part of the difficulty with cotton, tobacco, and wheat in the 'thirties can be traced to the self-sufficiency programmes of European countries.

These difficulties, in turn, lead to certain attitudes of farmers towards economic policy. First of all, there is a tendency — whether the word is used or not — for farmers to insist on "parity"; that is to say, on a given relationship between farm prices and other prices. Fortunately, farmers seldom insist on a given share of the national income. Any such request would be very difficult to meet because, as a country matures, it becomes more industrialized, and more people are engaged in providing services; as a result, the share of agriculture in the national income tends to be reduced. This decline in the relative position of agriculture does not create a very serious problem so long as the total economy is growing rapidly, for then the relative shift can be attained without reducing the size of the agricultural population. But when expansion of the economy begins to slow down, a relative decline in agriculture may mean that actual individuals, perhaps whole families, must move out of agriculture and into other occupations, if income per farm family is to continue rising. As Professor J. D. Black says: "In a growing economy like that of the United States of America, agriculture can scarcely hope to expand as fast as industry and trade. Hence its young people must move to the cities in large numbers."[8]

The necessity of a contraction in the relative share of agriculture in the national income with its concomitant "drift to the cities" when an economy is no longer growing at a fast rate causes resentment among farmers. This resentment expresses itself in the demand for "parity", and in efforts to organize. In the first instance, those efforts often take the form of co-operative organizations. When it is discovered that these are unable to protect all the interests of agriculture, farmers turn to politics, and organize pressure groups to bring their wishes directly to the notice of governments. Finally, farmers turn to restrictionism, designed to spread the needed contraction in agriculture among all existing farmers. During the interwar period, we observed the curious phenomenon of governments helping farmers to

8 J. D. Black, *Parity, Parity, Parity*, Cambridge (Mass) 1941, p. 108.

establish monopoly positions for themselves, which they were unable to establish with their own organizations. In 1934, one million American corn-hog farmers signed a contract with the Secretary of Agriculture, undertaking to reduce their corn acreage from 54 million to 41 million, while for their destructive actions—the Secretary of Agriculture agreed to pay them $320 million. N. S. B. Gras, in his book *A History of Agriculture,* says: "The souls of millions of litters of pigs rose in plaintive cry, and the souls of more millions merely stifled a sigh." The same sort of programme was introduced for cotton, wheat, tobacco and other products. Similar policies were pursued in the United Kingdom, Canada, and elsewhere.

The Farmers' Attitude Towards Economists

I am not sure that farmers have an "attitude" towards economists. Most farmers have only the vaguest of ideas as to what an economist is. If they do have an attitude, it is to trust those people whom they recognize as "farm economists", which usually means somebody born on a farm who now calls himself an economist. Certainly the farmer is reluctant to accept economics as "scientific", if it does not promise short-run gains to agriculture. A striking example of this reluctance is provided by the recent fracas at Iowa State College. A bulletin edited by Professor Theodore Schulz, then Professor of Economics at Iowa State, published an article stating that oleo-margarine compared favourably with butter in nutritional value. The Iowa dairy farmers brought so much organized pressure to bear on the University that Professor Schulz was asked to publish another article retracting the first one. Schulz refused, and resigned, together with some of the most distinguished members of his staff. Conflicts of this kind are apt to occur whenever farmers' interests seem endangered by something economists say.

The Economists' Attitude Towards Farmers

Economists are inclined to object to over-emphasis on farming as "a way of life". The farmer complains of his low income, but he is unwilling to (a) move, (b) change to new crops, (c) use new techniques, or (d) exploit subsidiary income opportunities. The refusal of the farmer to change his "way of life" may be defensible, but not when combined with the insistent pressure on governments to improve his standard of living.[9] The economist is also opposed to the use of political power to create monopoly positions for agriculture, and has a feeling that the farmer's concept of the "parity" or "normal" price is the highest price in the memory of living man.[10] Finally, the economist feels that the farmer takes too short-run a view, which leads to "mining" the soil, erosion, dust-bowls, and the like.

Conclusions

Professor J. D. Black asks[11] whether democracy can function with three such powerful groups as Big Business, Big Labour and Big Agriculture battling with each other:

[9] A colleague at McGill University, Professor Keirstead, tells a very nice story about a farmer in New Brunswick. This farmer had once operated a blacksmith's shop. During the war, the government sent a representative to persuade this farmer to undertake some sub-contracting on war supplies. The government official found the farm with some difficulty, and was greeted by the farmer's wife. "Where is Mr. MacDonald?" he asked. "Oh!" she replied, "you can't see him today; he's gone fishing." "Well, I have come over a thousand miles, from Ottawa, to see him on government business. Couldn't I go and look for him?" "Well," said she, "he won't like being interrupted, but if you go down this way for half a mile till you find the stream and then turn to the right and follow the stream for a mile — he fishes there." After a long walk and a difficult search the official found the farmer. "Mr. MacDonald . . . " he began. "Sh——!" said MacDonald, "there's a big fellow down there just about to bite; now please don't interrupt me!" The Ottawa official waited, shifting impatiently from one foot to another. After some time, he tried again. "Mr. MacDonald, I am a busy man and we have a proposition to make to you. We would like you to use your blacksmith's shop to make some parts for war supplies." "Oh, no!" said MacDonald: "I haven't been using that blacksmith's shop for a long time. I couldn't do that." "We are prepared to pay you very well for it," said the official. "Anyhow," said MacDonald, "I have no time; I have to look after the chickens." "But, Mr. MacDonald," said the official, "we would pay you far more than you could possibly hope to make out of your chickens; you could let the chickens go." "Oh!" said MacDonald, "I could never let the chickens go; I can't abide store eggs!"

[10] Professor J. D. Black expresses the view of most economists when he writes: "Production adjustment programs therefore should not be conceived of as increasing the total revenue from farm products by reducing their aggregate agricultural output year after year. Instead they should be directed towards smoothing out irregularities in supplies such as are produced by unusually good weather two years in succession, by production cycles, by over-responses to good prices and the like, and toward hastening readjustments made necessary by sudden developments such as invention of new farm machines, the opening of new production areas, unexpected loss of markets, business depressions, wars, and the like" (*op. cit.*, p. 213).

[11] *Ibid*, p. 4.

And so the forces of Agriculture now (May 1942) find themselves drawn up in battle formation and facing labour and
capital. Never before have the forces of agriculture been so
strongly mobilized in Congress and out. At times recently, it has
almost seemed as if the Farm Bloc was riding herd over Congress, the President of the United States, and the people of the
nation. . . . But labour is also powerfully organized and represented, and not merely in the halls of Congress. As for industry
and trade, they have behind them an older and better record
of successfully guarding and promoting their particular interests
than have agriculture and labour. Resources of wealth and gifted
personnel count mightily in a struggle of interests for advantage. Just at a time of great peril to the common cause for
which our great Union was conceived, witness these three forces
armed to the teeth and facing each other in Congress, in administrative parleys, in W.P.B. and O.P.A. conferences. If each group
were to be granted all that it asks, no one of them would get
more than a fraction at most of what it really seeks. . . . Meanwhile, the nation's great needs are met haltingly and late.

Professor Black points[12] to the grave danger of moral and
political breakdown under such conditions:

The ignoble fate of France in the past few years is plain for
all to see. The basis for this was laid in the twenty years before.
All of this time strong forces within struggled for control of
government, desiring to shape it to the ends of particular
interests. Each group insisted that the ends it sought were best
for the nation, too. Meanwhile the true best interests of France
triumphed only sporadically. . . . The British government was
functioning only a little better during the latter part of this
period. . . . There have been times when popular government has
largely failed even in these United States. One of those times
was in the last three years of the Hoover Administration. Yet the
Congress could take no useful action, tied hand and foot by
contending factions all looking mainly after their immediate
interests as they saw them. . . . To prevent a recurrence of such
a situation . . . the first requirement is a good understanding by
each group of the conditions within the other groups.

World War II is over, but the crisis of democracy is not.
Organization of politics around the "Big Three" economic
groups takes us a long step in the direction of the corporative state. Can an economy dominated by the Big Three be
efficient economically and democratic politically? The last
lecture will be concerned with this question.

---

12 *Ibid*, pp. 5-6.

VI

ETHICS, POLITICS, AND THE CRISIS OF DEMOCRACY

IN A BOOK ENTITLED *Swastika Night,* Murray Constantine envisages a world some centuries after an imagined Nazi victory in World War II. Feudalism has been restored; Hitler has been made a god; and all books have been destroyed except one, which is passed on secretly, generation by generation, from father to son. This book contains what was remembered of human history by a descendant of Hess, and is now in the possession of a German knight, whose name is von Hess. The knight has no son, and he has chosen a young Englishman, Alfred, to receive the book and preserve what is known of human history. At one point the knight and Alfred are discussing democracy:

"In a democracy no man is willing to give up his right of private judgment, and as he cannot blindly trust his leader, knowing him to be of the same clay as himself, he must be the leader. So government becomes exceedingly difficult. Because while there are many men of character, and democracy encourages them, there is also the large mass of weaker men, who must be told always what to do and what not to do, and cannot be trusted to live rightly without laws.

"So the end of democracy", von Hess says, "is always the same: it breaks up into chaos, and out of chaos comes some kind of authoritarian government, a Fuehrer, an oligarchy, government by the army, or something of the kind. Now I am not so contemptuous of democracy as he is, because I have seen the ultimate natural decay of authoritarian government, which is complete stagnation. But I still do not see how democracy can be made to last long enough to develop character in a sufficient number of people."

Alfred was deeply interested, frowning with concentration. "I don't think people ought to chuck — what did you call it — democracy, just because it's difficult", he said. "They ought to be so certain it's right that they can face any difficulties. If they persevered with it, it would get easier and easier, after a time. Did they ever try it for very long?"

In my first lecture, I asked: "Do economists know anything to eliminate or alleviate pervasive fears of inflation, unemployment, social conflict, revolution and war?" I answered that economists know enough to eliminate inflation and unemployment, to improve the allocation of resources, to maintain economic growth, and at the same time to reduce inequalities of income. In the second lecture, I defined certain areas of agreement and disagreement among economists, and contended that disagreements regarding questions on frontiers of knowledge, details of method, and politics, did not prevent economists from agreeing on specific measures for the achievement of clearly stated objectives. In the third lecture, I laid down a set of objectives of economic policy which would be non-controversial among people who would accept two basic value judgments — that it is good for people to be happy, and that people are made happier by having more goods and services and leisure to consume. In the fourth lecture, I showed how economic conflict, both internal and international, arose out of abuses of the freedom to exploit — the freedom to use one's bargaining power to the full — and indicated how unemployment and inflation in particular aggravate social conflict. I argued that the elimination of unemployment, inflation, monopoly exploitation of all kinds, and gross inequities of income distribution would virtually eliminate internal economic conflict and, by eliminating threats to particular economic and social systems from within, would also reduce the danger of war.

In the fifth lecture, I indicated a tendency in the western democracies for economic and political life to be dominated by the Big Three — Big Business, Big Labour and Big Agriculture. I pointed to certain ideological conflicts among the Big Three regarding economic policy, and raised the question whether democracy can work if the Big Three continue to use their economic and political bargaining power for selfish aims, especially to raise their respective share of the national income, and to enhance their prestige through control over the production and distribution of goods and services.

The subjects of these previous lectures transgress the borders of other social sciences, but are nevertheless subjects on which the economist may claim to have some special knowledge. This last lecture, however, penetrates fields of discussion where the tools of the economist fail completely. The best that can be said is that the economist is more keenly aware than others of the nature and complexity of economic problems and policies and may have some light to shed on the political and ethical problems that surround them.

If we are to discuss the "crisis" of democracy, we must first ask: "What is democracy?" This question is by no means a simple one. UNESCO recently circulated a questionnaire among some five hundred historians and scientists, philosophers, jurists, and economists. The replies indicate agreement that democracy is a good thing, and agreement that democracy means, in some sense, rule of the people by themselves in their own interest. But there the agreement ends. There is violent disagreement as to who "the people" are and what constitutes the "interest" of the people.

We must avoid defining democracy in such a way as to make it synonymous with capitalism or with socialism. Schumpeter — no friend of socialism — points out towards the end of his book, *Capitalism, Socialism, and Democracy*:[1]

Between socialism as we defined it and democracy as we defined it, there is no necessary relation: the one can exist without the other. At the same time, there is no incompatibility: in appropriate states of the social environment the socialist engine can be run on democratic principles.

At the same time, we must not identify democracy with socialism. One hundred years ago Alexis de Tocqueville told the Assemblée Constituante:

No, gentlemen, democracy and socialism are not necessarily inter-connected. They are not only different — they are opposed. Are you perchance trying to tell me that democracy consists in the creation of a more vexatious, more meddlesome and more restrictive form of government than any other, with the sole difference that you let the people elect it and make it act in the name of the people? But then what would you have done but confer on tyranny an air of legality which it did not possess and ensure for it the force and independence it lacked. Democracy extends the sphere of individual independence, socialism contracts it. Democracy gives to every man his full value, socialism makes of every man an agent, an instrument, a cipher. Demo-

1 London 1947, p. 284.

cracy and socialism are linked only by the word "equality"; but note the difference. Democracy wants equality in freedom, socialism wants equality in constraint and enslavement.[2]

The UNESCO survey turned up the usual distinction between proletarian and bourgeois democracy. The contrast between these two concepts of democracy was especially sharply drawn in the reply of Professor Charles Bettelheim of the University of Paris:[3]

Bourgeois democracy is a democracy for the bourgeoisie and a dictatorship for the proletariat. When bourgeois democracy is in its most democratic guise, this dictatorship takes the form, essentially, of an ideological dictatorship; it imposes on the proletariat (by means of the school, the church, the press, radio, film, etc.) views and ideals designed to maintain the supremacy of the bourgeoisie. But the weapons of material, violent dictatorship — the police, army, law courts and prisons — are always ready to hand, and are resorted to whenever the proletariat, as for instance on the occasion of a strike, strays from the path which the bourgeoisie wants it to follow. They are also resorted to when the ideological dictatorship is weakening and the proletariat subscribes to an ideology other than that of the bourgeoisie; the latter then attempts to substitute open dictatorship for the former masked dictatorship, and bourgeois democracy disappears. Proletarian democracy, in its turn, is a democracy for the proletariat, and a dictatorship for the bourgeoisie.

Similarly, Bertrand Russell says:[4]

The Anglo-Saxon definition of "democracy" is that it consists in the rule of the majority; the Russian view is that it consists in the interests of the majority, these interests being determined in accordance with Marxist political philosophy.

Admitting, then, that the term is not one that is easily defined, I shall, nevertheless, lay down certain criteria which, I think, indicate the presence of democracy. There are, first, certain attributes of democratic political organization: governments must be elected by periodic free elections, with suffrage limited only by age; there must be rule by law, the laws must be passed by a majority of the elected representatives, and force must be used only against those who break the law; and there must be effective machinery through

---

2 Quoted in UNESCO *Philosophical Analysis of Current Ideological Conflicts*, P.H.S. 10, Annex iii, p. 7.
3 UNESCO *Courier*, May 1949.
4 *What is Democracy?* London 1946, p. 14.

which the wishes of the electorate can be translated into government action.

Secondly, there are certain attributes of the social organization of democracy. These include the freedoms of speech, press, assembly and worship. I am inclined to think, too, that true democracy requires equal access for all political parties to the channels through which public opinion is formed. I recall a meeting of the Canadian Manufacturing Association at which the leading speaker was the President of the U.S. National Association of Manufacturers. He was pleading for a united front of Canadian and American businessmen to fight all forms of government intervention. "Mark my words", he said. "In the final analysis Communism, Socialism and a managed capitalism are the same thing. In the United States of America", he continued, "the business community are mobilizing the press, movies, radio, schools and pulpits to fight all three — including the New Deal." Where it is possible for such mobilization of the organs of public opinion to take place, can true democracy prevail?

Finally, there is a certain philosophical content in democracy. It includes, I think, the concept of respect for the dignity of the individual. The State, in a true democracy, is regarded as a collection of individuals, and not as something which has a life of its own. True democracy also includes the values which Professor Northrop has described as the Latin concept of freedom — respect of the right of the individual to make his own choices on matters of taste, opinion, belief and behaviour not specifically covered by law. If you like, this freedom could be called the "freedom for eccentricity".

Where can we find examples of democracy thus defined? Obviously, nowhere. But obviously, too, the "western democracies" (including Australia, Belgium, Canada, France, Holland, the United Kingdom, the United States of America, Norway, Sweden, and Switzerland) come closest to the situation described above.

What, then, is the "crisis" of democracy? The answer to this question should be clear from the argument of the preceding lectures. The crisis arises out of the struggle of the Big Three — Big Business, Big Labour and Big Agriculture — for a larger share of the national income, for security, and for the prestige that goes with the control over the production and distribution of goods and services. This battle among the Big Three tends to lead to deadlock in the economic policy of the western democracies, because it is virtually impossible to introduce and administer any policy if it encounters strong opposition from any one of the major groups. Consequently, there is a danger that economic policy in the democracies will fail to maintain full employment, prevent inflation, improve the income distribution, and so on, so that social conflict will be intensified and the danger of revolution enhanced.

There is also the danger of drifting into the Corporative State in the western democracies, without even an integrated Fascist ideology to make it function. As Professor Röpke says in his recent book:[5]

Has there ever been so much lack of character, so little civil courage, so much conformity and cynical opportunism, so many weak knees as in our generation. If there be any exaggeration in this view, it may well be excused when we take contemporary events into account, events which are visible to every observer and which provide us with a highly depressing general picture. We are unable to comprehend the history of recent decades unless we know that there has taken place an unbelievable shifting towards collectivism, regimentation of opinion, socialization of existence and an abandonment of personality passing through every stage of mere wavering of judgment to reluctant submission to the most shameless opportunism. It would seem as though men who, in the mass in their contempt of physical death have almost put their ancestors in the shade, have simultaneously unlearnt that other individual form of bravery which we designate civil courage, and this fact corroborates our general diagnosis of the disease of our society.

The control of economic and political life by Big Business, Big Labour and Big Agriculture takes us a long step in the direction of corporative state.

Moreover, spectacular failure of economic policy in the western democracies could lead to ideological defeat of democracy in the rest of the world. An ideological defeat of

---

5 Wilhelm Röpke, *Civitas Humana*, London 1948, p. 99.

the western democracies would divide the world into Communist countries and Fascist countries, thus intensifying the ideological conflict in the world as a whole. We must not under-estimate the strength of the Marxist and Fascist ideologies, which provide banners behind which people can march better than any that liberalism has yet provided. A dramatic economic failure in the western democracies in the near future is more likely to lead to some species of Fascism in the western democracies themselves than to some species of Communism. Thus a dramatic failure would leave the entire world divided into two ideologically hostile camps. It is highly unlikely that such a world could live in peace.

There is also a strong likelihood that democracy would be defeated, even if capitalism wins, in a fight between the western democracies and Russia. We fought one war to make the world safe for democracy. It made the world safe for Fascism in western Europe and for Communism in eastern Europe. We fought a second world war to defeat Fascism. It resulted in the spread of Communism to formerly democratic countries, while in other countries Fascist ideologies seem stronger than ever. If we are to fight Russia, we will need an intensification of economic and political control which will leave us, even in the event of victory, with a political economy which is even less democratic than the one we now have.

Is there no economic system which will, by itself, guarantee us the attainment of the economic objectives laid down within a political framework which is "democratic" as defined above?

Let us consider the three most clamorous claimants of our time — Communism, Fascism, and *Laissez-faire*. Communism cannot be dismissed as undemocratic *in itself,* just because the present Communist countries do not meet the criteria of democracy laid down above. A possible line of attack would be to preach Communism to democracies, and democracy to Communist countries, until we have democratic Communism the world over, thus resolving international conflicts.

Nor can Communism be dismissed as inherently unethical.

The ultimate objective of Communism is virtually unassailable from an ethical viewpoint: an economy of such abundance that no economic conflicts arise between individuals or groups; a classless society in which the coercive power of the state is totally unnecessary, and in which everyone contributes what he can to national income and takes what he needs from it. Lenin has described the ultimate aim of Communism as follows:[6]

We set ourselves the ultimate aim of abolishing the state, i.e. all organized and systematic violence, all use of violence against man in general. We do not expect the advent of an order of society in which the principle of the subordination of the minority to the majority will not be observed. But in striving for Socialism we are convinced that it will develop into Communism, and, hence, that the need for violence against people in general, the need for the subjection of one man to another, and of one section of the population to another, will vanish, since people will become accustomed to observing the elementary conditions of social life without force and without subordination.

How very ethical it sounds!

David McCord Wright, who has recently won the acclaim of the United States Chamber of Commerce for his book on *Democracy and Progress,* writes:[7]

Prima facie the Communist gospel accepts nearly all of our highest values, and its relation to the ideals of the eighteenth century *illuminati* is obvious. Men are naturally "good" and naturally "equal". Evil and inequality spring alike from a "bad" environment. If, with the aid of "science" we create a "good" environment, men will become "good", and so on.

Why, then, should we reject the Communist solution? I believe there are good reasons for fighting Communism, at least until the movement is rescued from its present revolutionary Marxist leaders. The reasons are these:

The frictionless, classless anarchy is a very long-run goal, and meanwhile the Communist state is to be subjected to a

---

[6] Lenin, "The State and Revolution", in *The Essentials of Lenin,* London 1946, ii. 197.

[7] David McCord Wright, "The Economics of a Classless Society", *American Economic Review, Supplement,* May 1949, pp. 27-8.

Wysten Auden writes, "Communism is the only political theory that really holds the Christian position of absolute equality in value of every individual, and the evil of all State restraint" (Lewis, Polanyi, and Kitchin, editors, *Christianity and the Social Revolution,* London 1935, p. 49). Similar statements by clerical writers can be found in the same volume.

THE CRISIS OF DEMOCRACY

"dictatorship of the proletariat", which in practice would mean dictatorship by the leaders of the revolutionary movement and their successors. These leaders would be unlikely to achieve the economic objectives laid down within the democratic framework. Few of them really accept the political freedoms of western democracy as desirable ends. They want political freedom only for people who agree with them. True, most people do; let's admit it. In the United States of America today we see an organized effort to curtail the freedom of those who dislike the existing economic and social order. But, even in the United States of America today, there seems to be a good deal more freedom for the opposition than there is in the Soviet Union; at least the *principle* of freedom of speech, thought, assembly and election is upheld.

Moreover, few of the leaders of the Communist movement have the slightest conception of the complexities of economic planning in a socialist state; they swallow the bad with the good in Marxist economics and reject all other economics; they are consequently ill-equipped to plan socialist societies. It is possible, of course, that they may run an economy better than it is being run at present, but because of the limitations in their economic training and outlook they will not run it as well as it *could be* run.

Finally, the leaders are motivated as much by hatred and desire for revenge as by love for their fellow men, and would consequently tend to destroy too much that is useful or desirable in present society. As Professor Knight has put it: "If the gospel of love will not solve our problems, we must admit the fact and turn from it in sorrow, but we can both confidently and joyfully reject the gospel of hate."

Let us have a brief look at Fascism. Fascist literature reveals two distinct and contradictory attitudes towards democracy. In some Fascist literature democracy is described as decadent. Some literature, however, argues that Fascism is "democracy in practice". People's political interests, the argument goes, are really a reflection of their economic interests, and they can express those economic and political interests better as members of an economic group than they can as members of a political party. Therefore, these Fascist theorists say, let us scrap the outmoded party system, and organize a political system in terms of economic groups — corporatives — and let people vote for their representatives, not as members of a party, but as members of a labour group, or an agricultural group, or an employers' group, and so on. This is not very far, you see, from the sort of situation for which we are heading in any case.

It is important too, I think, to divorce the theory of the corporative state, and the ethics of the corporative state as laid down in the "Quadrigesimo Anno", from the actual régimes of Hitler and Mussolini. So many things happened under Fascism which we intensely disliked that it is hard to think clearly about the implications of the corporative state as such. Are such things as race-prejudice, domination by the owner-class, and the police-state, *inherent* in the corporative form of organization? We have not yet digested the corporative state. We need to think it through. May not the consecration of the individual to the state be ethically superior to crass, egocentric materialism? As Professor Keirstead has said:[8]

The ethics of modern business enterprise is an ignoble one. Anything goes. People may be bullied, brow-beaten, frightened, cajoled into buying things they neither need nor want. Public taste may be degraded, public morality corrupted, to serve the ends of profit and power. The acquisitive instinct is nurtured to the exclusion of all others. The value system of a whole society, its entire culture, reflects the baseness of taste, the ignobility and venality of those men who set its tone and whose own standards are fixed and qualities determined by the necessities of the commercial world. No one can seriously maintain that this halting and inadequate organization of our economy, with its topsy-turvy scheme of values, its base, ignorant and uncultivated aristocracy, and its growing menace of concentrated and irresponsible power is an end in itself, a social good in its own right to be retained at whatever cost to social security and human welfare.

Also, Professor Knight, who is perhaps the staunchest defender of *laissez-faire* among leading contemporary American economists, says:[9]

---

8 B. S. Keirstead, *The Theory of Economic Change,* Toronto 1948, pp. 327-8.
9 F. H. Knight, *The Ethics of Competition,* p. 65.

Successful business men have not become proverbial for the qualities that the best minds and most sensitive spirits of the race agree in calling noble. Business as it is and has been does not commonly display a very high order of sportsmanship, not to mention the question which will be raised presently as to whether sportsmanship itself is the highest human ideal.

In contrast with the actual practical ethics of the western democracies, the ethics which subordinates the individual to the state does not come off too badly.

I believe, nevertheless, that the Fascist solution should also be rejected. First of all, it is not sufficient to set up a boxing ring within which conflicts can be settled according to Marquess of Queensberry rules, which is what the corporative state does in theory. It does not try to *solve* basic conflicts. It admits the presence of conflict and says: "We cannot allow this conflict to disrupt society." The result is state control. It says: "We will lay down a set of rules, and will set up some institution to see that that strife is carried out under the supervision of a referee." In this sense, the Australian Arbitration Court, and the Industrial Working Parties in the United Kingdom, are Fascist institutions; that is to say, they are tripartite organizations — the employers confront the employees, and the government acts as referee.[10] This is the essential theory of the corporative state. It does not eliminate conflict; it only prevents conflict from breaking out into open violence.

Secondly, the Fascist solution must be rejected because there is no acceptable Fascist leadership. Fascist leaders and intellectuals have provided no convincing evidence that they are interested either in the achievement of the economic objectives outlined above, or in the maintenance of democracy as defined here. There is good reason to doubt that the potential leaders of any new Fascist movement would have popular interests in mind. There is also reason to suspect that they know even less about the problems of managing an economy than the Communist leaders. Fascist economic theory is just as antagonistic to *laissez-faire* as Communist

---

10 The International Labour Organization is similarly constituted, and nearly all western democracies have such tripartite institutions.

theory, but when it comes to a positive solution, it becomes even more illogical and breaks down even more completely.

Finally, I have a suspicion that the corporative state and domination by an *élite* are closely connected. They have certainly been connected historically, and I am inclined to think that a political system which demarcates people into hostile groups, and leaves the government to make final decisions in the conflicts among those groups, will inevitably produce one group which will run the government in its own way, and so run the economy as a whole.

Return to Laissez-faire?

There are two groups of proponents of a return to *laissez-faire*. Some of them want to legislate the conditions of perfect competition, so that the economy can proceed under rule by law, without administrative direction by government officials.[11] Others want true *laissez-faire,* in the sense of a simple "hands-off" policy. Complete *laissez-faire* in this latter sense has never existed — not even as an ideal in the economic literature — and a movement in that direction now would be completely counter to current trends. With the trend towards bigger firms, together with the growth of technical knowledge and managerial skill, the most efficient size of firms gets bigger and bigger. Labour and agriculture, too, are becoming increasingly aware of the advantages of large-scale organization.

More important, a mere "hands-off" policy of government would make economic conditions worse rather than better. It would lead to a still more haphazard income distribution, by removing such curbs to ruthless exploitation of superior bargaining positions as now exist. The removal of restraints on monopolies — including labour and agricultural monopolies as well as business monopolies — would worsen the allocation of resources as well. As for full employment with-

---

11 "Rule of Law" is used in the narrow sense of Dicey's formulation in Chapter IV of his classic *Law of the Constitution.* It is highly doubtful whether this formulation is acceptable in a modern democratic state. Cf. W. Friedmann, *The Planned State and the Rule of Law,* Melbourne 1948, especially pp. 9-22.

out inflation, there is little reason to suppose that *laissez-faire* capitalism would work better in the future than it has done in the past, and there are very good reasons for supposing that it would work worse, with the weakening of the forces of capitalist expansion. Population growth is tapering off, frontiers are disappearing, innovations are becoming capital-releasing rather than capital-absorbing. Outlets for investment are growing less fast than before, while personal and institutional savings continue to grow as fast as ever. The result is a chronic tendency in advanced countries towards an excess of savings over investments at high levels of unemployment. This tendency is interrupted only by inflationary booms, and even these are largely confined to war and immediate post-war periods. Economic progress is stultified by chronic unemployment, by misdirection of investment in inflation, and by wastage of resources through short-run planning for individual gain, as distinct from long-run planning for the net social advantage.

The proponents of a return to complete *laissez-faire* by "legislating" competition, on the other hand, grossly underestimate the political and economic problems involved in creating by law anything vaguely resembling the perfectly competitive economy of the textbook, the efficacy of which is the sole foundation of *laissez-faire* economic philosophy. It is worth recalling what "perfect competition" entails. It means that no firm, farmer, or worker, and no organization of firms, farmers, and workers, is large or powerful enough to affect in the slightest degree the price of anything it buys or sells. It means that the price of every commodity and every factor of production is adjusted immediately to any change in demand for it or cost of it. It means perfect knowledge by all buyers and sellers of all opportunities in the market, and an ability to appraise accurately the quality of goods and services offered. It means perfect foresight, or complete and costless mobility of all factors of production, so that mistakes never bring losses — or profits. The proposal to return to *laissez-faire* in the sense of legislating for perfect competition is conservative in wishing to retain rule by law, instead of rule by the bureaucrats of government, business and labour; but it is radical in the extreme in terms of the revolution in economic organization that would be needed to implement it.

The Need for a "Mixed" System

The conclusion of this brief survey of Communism, Fascism, and Laissez-faire seems clear: *no* politico-economic system will, in itself, guarantee the achievement of the economic objectives laid down, within a democratic political framework. *Nothing* will do this job but knowledge and good will. From the technical point of view, a mixed economic system in which a certain amount of continuous government management of the economy is undertaken, while large areas of economic choice are left to individuals and groups, offer us most hope of success.

It is appropriate to think of possible systems that might be substituted for the present one, including centralized collectivism, decentralized collectivism, and — in some ways most radical of all — a return to a system of thorough-going competition between large numbers of independent producing units. But these alternatives are not live issues for us today. They are either things we cannot have or things most of us do not want. Contemplation of them serves mainly to clarify the limits between which we must steer, on the course that lies inevitably before us. On the whole, it seems truer to say that there is only one possible system: the system of using the agencies that exist and trying to make them work together. This means a mixed system.[12]

A mixed system, however, intensifies the inherent economic conflicts, and the related political conflicts, among the major economic groups. Such a system, therefore, requires certain improvements in the governmental process.

Political Problems of a Mixed Economy

There are two possible approaches to the problem of political organization in a mixed economy. Schumpeter proposes giving up any effort to find the "common will" and defining democracy as a system that provides the people with a mechanism for choosing political leaders, who will decide what the problems are and how they will be solved:[13]

---

12 J. M. Clark, *Alternative to Serfdom,* Oxford 1948, p. 123.
13 *Op. cit.,* pp. 269-71.

To put it differently, we now take the view that the role of the people is to produce a government, or else an intermediate body which in turn will produce a national executive or government. And we define: the democratic method is that institutional arrangement for arriving at political decisions in which individuals acquire the power to decide by means of a competitive struggle for the people's vote. Defense and explanation of this idea will speedily show that, as to both plausibility of assumption and tenability of propositions, it greatly improves the theory of the democratic process. First of all, we are provided with a reasonably efficient criterion by which to distinguish democratic governments from others. . . . Second, the theory embodied in this definition leaves all the room we may wish to have for a proper recognition of the vital fact of leadership. . . . Third, however, so far as there are genuine group-wise volitions at all, for instance the will of the unemployed to receive unemployment benefit or the will of other groups to help — our theory does not neglect them. On the contrary we are now able to insert them in exactly the role which they actually play. Such volitions do not as a rule assert themselves directly. Even if strong and definite they remain latent, often for decades, until they are called to life by some political leader who turns them into political factors.

This approach seems defeatist. A second approach is to try to determine the popular will, but to abandon the idea that periodic elections alone provide an adequate means of expressing popular will. This approach may require some modification of the party system. A multi-party system leads to paralysis. On the other hand, a two-party system leads to political agglomeration; each party tends to move as close to the other as it can, in order to get as many votes as possible. Moreover, the concept of inevitable conflict between "government" and "opposition" parties prevents good economic policy from being adopted and confuses the electorate. If we are to have effective economic policy, there must be many occasions on which government and opposition agree, in peacetime as in war. If the opposition feel obliged to take a position contrary to the government's on every question of economic policy that occurs, the problems associated with a mixed economy will never be solved. Such agreement may mean — as it did during the war — that the means of expressing political views cannot be reduced by voting for one party rather than the other. More use of the referendum is one device that suggests itself. Under modern methods of polling, it does not take very long to hold a referendum and count the votes. A more or less continuous process of testing public opinion on economic policy questions would greatly increase the efficiency of the government so far as economic policy is concerned, while maintaining an essentially demo- cratic form.

General elections cannot isolate the electorate's views as to the relative importance, let us say, of full employment with- out inflation, and a more equal income distribution. How- ever, more use of the referendum will mean that the power to phrase questions will be an extremely important political power, since the answers to a referendum depend a good deal on how the questions are phrased. Perhaps the official opposition party should agree to the form in which the question is put.

The original United States Full Employment Bill of 1945 is worthy of careful study in connection with the general problem of making democracy work well in the economic sphere. It was an effort to define the scope of administrative discretion. While other measures of control were kept in the hands of the legislature, the executive branch of the govern- ment was given power to make certain fundamental decisions without referring to the legislature — decisions on tax rates and current rates of expenditure, within limits imposed by the budget approved by the legislature. These provisions were thrown out of the final Act, but the original Bill, I think, suggested certain ways in which the political system could be modified to permit a greater degree of flexibility of economic policy while retaining the ultimate control for the legislature.

Another needed reform is the provision of expert advice to opposition parties at public expense. In these days, when the process of government consists so largely of legislating and administering economic policy, having a body of experts at its beck and call is a big advantage for the party in power. True, the opposition may ask questions in the House, or may send the appropriate Minister a request for certain information; but the government retains the right *not* to give information on certain subjects, and can always say, "not available". This problem could be solved by setting up a Civil Service at the disposal of opposition parties.

Ethical Problems in a Mixed Economy

With all these devices, and any other devices that might be thought up for increasing the economic efficiency of democratic government, no democracy will work well unless the Big Three can reach some understanding with regard to national policy. If each of the Big Three — no matter how well-informed — continues to pursue its own selfish aims, I do not think that democratic government can operate efficiently for very long.

The trouble is that most people in the western world divorce economics from ethics in their thinking. Business is business, a strike is a strike, farm subsidies are farm subsidies, while morality is something entirely different. As Professor Knight says:[14]

An outstanding ethical consequence of the theory of productive organization through freeing the urge to self-advancement is a new and sharp division in the field of conduct, a new ethical dualism (there are many such dualisms) or at least a bifurcation of the ethical problem. The situation is suggested by the vernacular expression "business is business", meaning that business is one thing, and charity another. There is a strong feeling that it is "right" to play the business game according to the rules, to make exchanges at the ratios objectively set or made possible by the market. That is, it is assumed to be ethically legitimate and even positively virtuous, to desire to maximize one's income, as defined above, and to act in such a way as to do so, subject always to the sweeping reservation of mutual free consent in all relations with others.

The principle of "business is business" is on a par with that of "justice is blind", though both must be sometimes seasoned with mercy. Moral obligation to persons in consequence of special relationships is the general principle of feudalism, and is anachronistic and disruptive in a commercial or enterprise economy. Yet it persists; and not only in connection with the employer-employee relation; it, or its conflict with business principles and with wide areas of law as a whole, remains a fundamental aspect

---

14 F. H. Knight, "Ethics and Economic Reform", *Economica*, February 1949, pp. 12-16.

of the ethical problem-situation in modern society. The mixture of intellectual confusion with value judgments in the discussion of problems of economic ethics, as it takes place, baffles analysis, and is of course most sinister in import.

This divorce of ethics from economics is not the fault of economists. The economist has always been interested in ethical problems. Indeed, economics is as much an offshot of moral philosophy as it is of any branch of knowledge. Adam Smith, too often remembered as the father of *laissez-faire* and for his statements regarding the invisible hand, was, in fact, an economic interventionist of the first order. He approved minimum wage legislation, legal limitations on profits, progressive income tax, price ceilings on necessities, smashing of monopolies, curtailment of exploitation by landlords, and extension of public enterprise to fields of social importance which are not, or should not be allowed to become, profitable for private enterprise.[15]

It is true that in the late nineteenth and early twentieth centuries, social criticism by orthodox economists was at a low ebb. This lapse of vituperation on the part of economists was partly the result of admiration for the rapid improvement in living standards that capitalism had brought about between 1850 and 1913. It was partly a reaction to the fuzziness of much of the socialist criticism, and partly the product of a childish delight in the elegance and symmetry of their pure theory of pure competition, a theory which was too seldom contrasted with the real world in which they were living. Even the liberal economists of the late nineteenth and early twentieth centuries were interventionists in considerable degree; they insisted on elimination of monopoly of all kinds and rigorous control of the credit mechanism. However, they felt that the shortcomings of the capitalist system could be remedied by passing and enforcing the right laws, especially anti-trust, banking and tax laws.

These bright dreams have been shattered by the events of the last thirty years. The succession of war, inflation, depres-

---

15 Cf. William D. Grampp, "On the Politics of the Classical Economist", *Quarterly Journal of Economics*, November 1948.

sion, war and inflation, has been too sharp a contrast to accepted objectives of economic policy for anyone to feel complacent about the functioning of our western social system. Moreover, the revolutions in economic thought during the 1930's destroyed any illusions about the facility with which these objectives could be attained. The theory of monopolistic competition, developed in the decade after 1931, has shown all too conclusively that pure competition is the exception rather than the rule. The theory of employment developed since 1936 has shown equally clearly why full employment without inflation does not occur very often in a private enterprise economy.

What is needed, I think, is a breaking down of the artificial distinction between economics and ethics among the general public. The business man must not be allowed to feel that he is virtuous merely because he restrains his drinking and his flirtation on Saturday night, and goes to Church on Sunday, if on Monday he hires thugs to break up a picket line, or makes a price-fixing agreement with a rival firm, or organizes a lobby to press for tax-cuts in an inflationary period. He must be considered a sinner, not only by workers, but by other business men as well; and he must be taught to regard himself as immoral. Similarly, the trade union official who, in a period of critical shortages, calls a strike merely because he fears that accumulation of inventories will impair his bargaining power, must be treated as immoral by all groups of society. The farmer who, through his co-operative, withholds produce from the market when people are starving, must be taught that he is a sinner; and so forth. As a concrete example, what is needed is more behaviour like that of the British Trades Union Congress, in supporting the government's proposals for wage stops to relieve inflationary pressure.

Does this recommendation boil down to an extension or resurgence of Christianity? Elsewhere, I have argued that it does, since what is needed is simply an extension of the "golden rule" to relationships between groups as well as between persons. Christ, I insisted, was far more concerned with social ethics, as distinct from personal ethics, than the Christian church seems to have been in recent decades.[16] This view certainly has its supporters. Thornton W. Merriam, for example, seems to regard Christianity as fundamentally a programme of social reform, along lines very similar to those suggested above.[17] Many theosophers consider Jesus to have been primarily a social agitator.[18] But some distinguished social philosophers take the opposite view. Knight, for example, insists that the Christian church has always played a reactionary role, and that it is unlikely to provide leadership for social reform in future. Moreover, he argues, the Christian ethic provides no guide to social action, and often conflicts with liberal ideals. In Knight's opinion, it is more important to be of the right mind than to be of the right heart.[19] "If civilization is destroyed," he maintains, "it will be through the misdirected effort to make it better, and not through passive indifference or deliberate rejection."[20] It must not be forgotten, either, that Christianity is not the only religion in which consideration for one's fellows is a fundamental principle.

The question as to what label best suits a society in which the cardinal ethical principle is that everyone, both as an individual and as a leader or member of an economic group, should do as he would be done by, is of secondary importance. We can surely all agree that ignorant men of good will can be dangerous, but that wise men of bad faith are much more dangerous. We can surely agree too that the right mind *and* the right heart are needed, if democracy is to perform well from the economic viewpoint.

If we fail to develop a society in which the actions of major economic groups is sincerely and intelligently directed

---

16 B. Higgins, "Economics and Ethics", *Australasian Journal of Philosophy*, August 1949. A *New Yorker* cartoon pictures a (presumably Anglican) bishop telling a hopeful young prelate, "If you want to succeed in this game, keep away from two subjects — politics and religion."
17 F. H. Knight and T. W. Merriam, *The Economic Order and Religion*, London, 1948.
18 See, for example, Conrad Noel, "Jesus", in Lewis, Polanyi, and Kitchin, *op. cit.*, pp. 60-69.
19 Knight and Merriam, *op. cit.*
20 *Ibid*, p. 57.

towards the common weal, we shall end up with an undemocratic political framework, and an economy that works very little better, and possibly even worse than the one which we have at present.[21] Moreover, as Professor Fred. Watkins warns at the end of his penetrating study of modern liberalism, "In a world living under the daily threat of military destruction the time available for liberal experimentation is dangerously short. If liberal statesmen fail in the near future to satisfy the prevailing hunger for economic and military security, the masses of mankind will turn with relief to the apparent simplicity and certainty of dictatorial solutions."[22]

The Economist in a Mixed Economy

What is the proper role of the professional economist in a democratic society with a "mixed" economy, in which the task of management is shared by government, business, labour, and agriculture?

The first duty of the economist is *to teach;* to teach economics to students, to business men, to farmers, to workers, and to the general public. The American Economic Association recently set up a committee on the teaching of economics, with the object of finding out the "purpose" of

21 "From this standpoint, it is curious that some will argue that only a belief in God can make democracy reasonable, while others argue with equal conviction that only by shifting our focus from God to man can we lay a sound basis for real democracy. And to each the bearing of his religious or anti-religious position on democracy is at least an added recommendation for it, in his eyes. But if people can agree on the desirability of democracy, who disagree on philosophy and religion, then is it possible that faith in humanity and democracy may be a better common denominator for a 'unified culture', and a more promising place to begin working toward it? One knows nominally Christian sects that lack this faith, and nominal atheists who possess it. The normal view seems to be that of the late Lord Tweedsmuir, who held it very important that a man have a philosophy, but less important what that philosophy should be. Or, in terms of our previous discussion, the fact that man is a social animal goes deeper in his nature than the rationalizations that he builds around it, to place it in his scheme of values or to connect it with things beyond the direct range of experience and observation.

"Be that as it may, for our present purpose we need to agree on one thing: respect for the worth and dignity of men and their need and duty to work together in a society, contributing to the common enterprise and restraining impulses to aggression and exploitation — one's own as well as those of others" (J. M. Clark, *op cit.,* p. 119).

22 *The Political Tradition of the West: a Study in the Development of Modern Liberalism,* Cambridge (Mass), 1948, p. 368.

courses in economics. Professor Kenneth Boulding made a
revolutionary suggestion: that the purpose of courses in economics is to teach economics, and not to teach "good citizen-
ship", "intelligent voting", or anything else. He is right. It is
essential, if we are to have a smooth-working economy within
a democratic political framework, to have an economically
sophisticated electorate. The only way to produce such an
electorate is to teach it economics.

In particular, teaching in Schools of Commerce and Agriculture should be broadened. Students in agriculture and
commerce need a solid grounding in general economics. They
also need to learn a professional ethics based not on loyalty
to their own group but on responsibility to society as a
whole; but I am not sure that economists are particularly
well qualified to teach ethics.

We also need trade union schools. A start has been made
in this direction in the United States of America. Harvard,
for example, has set up a school to train trade union leaders
in economics. Opposition to such training schools from
leaders of other groups is the height of short-sighted selfishness. How could anyone think that educated trade union
leaders would be more damaging to society than uneducated
ones?

The second function of economists is *to advise;* to advise
governments and opposition parties, to advise business, agricultural organizations, and — if advice is sought — to advise
individual business men, farmers and workers. As Professor
Gambs has pointed out:[23]

First of all, the world cannot afford to lose the journeyman
economist, whether as a civil servant or as a private citizen;
neither will the economist gain by withdrawing from the world
of affairs and taking to his tower of ivory. Proposed social and
economic legislation must be scrutinized, its repercussions fore-
seen, and, if adopted, its results observed, analysed, and recorded.
Only economists are competent to do such jobs — the thousand
and one jobs of rural, urban, state, and national housekeeping.
With all their faults, they are the only persons sufficiently
divorced from the special interests of the ironmonger, hog-
grower, truck driver, or brush salesman to be able to see, as

---

23 J. S. Gambs, *op. cit.,* p. 88.

Marshall puts it, "the one in the many and the many in the one". The world would fall apart if these artisan services were withdrawn, and theory would become sterile if theorists had no contact with reality.

Thirdly, I am inclined to think that economists have a responsibility *to preach*. Some might ask: "Why should economists make recommendations for policy at all?" If they content themselves with explaining economic phenomena, and analysing the effects of various policy proposals without judging them, could they not avoid expressing value judgments altogether? I believe the answer to this question is "No", for three rather different sorts of reasons. For one thing, it is doubtful whether economists could make a useful selection of phenomena, or devise methods of dealing with them, without some kind of economic problem in mind. Can you think of a single major advance in economic knowledge which was not the result — directly or indirectly — of an effort to find the solution to a social problem? The major advances of the last twenty years have been the theory of imperfect and monopolistic competition, which developed out of an effort to solve the monopoly problem, and the theory of income and employment determination, which arose from the endeavour to solve the problem of unemployment.

Now, once economists say that monopoly and unemployment are "problems", for which solutions should be sought, the value judgments have already been made. In other words, value judgments inform analysis. It would be possible, of course, to scrap the value judgments and keep the scientific principles after the analysis is finished; but some value judgments are necessary to get started.

Moreover, if analysis is undertaken, policy implications are inevitable. Are economists to form a secret society and reveal their results only to each other, under an oath of secrecy? If not, someone will infer policy implications from economic analysis and make propaganda of them. Government policy is always based on some kind of economic theory; and it had better be based on good economic theory. If economists do not interpret the policy implications of their own analysis, their scientific conclusions are liable to gross misinterpretation, either because they are imperfectly understood, or because particular individuals or groups wish to use them unscrupulously for their own purposes.

Finally, economics is an art as well as a science, and economists are people as well as scientists. Most economists, as people and as practitioners of the art of economics, really believe the two basic ethical premises outlined in my third lecture. They believe that people are made happier by having more goods and services and leisure to consume; and they believe that it is good for people to be happy. If they believe these things, economists are morally obliged to make recommendations of policy. As well ask the medical doctor why he makes prescriptions, instead of confining himself to diagnosis and prognosis, as to ask the economist why he succumbs to the temptation to formulate policy!

The final obligation of an economist in a mixed economy is *to learn*. The economist needs to learn a good deal about related social sciences. Team work among social scientists is necessary, in defining the scope, and choosing the simplifying assumptions to be used, for each of the respective fields. Team work is necessary again at the final stage, for formulating policy. Economists cannot formulate policy alone.

The economist also needs to learn much more about social change. If social change is to be guided, it has to be understood. If the Marxist theory of social change is wrong, what is right? The lack of an answer to this question is the most glaring of the gaps in systematic economic knowledge.

If he is to fulfil his obligations in a mixed economy, the economist must also be accorded certain rights. One thing the economist needs in a mixed economy is research funds with no strings attached. In the last fifteen years economic theory has made more progress than it had done for the previous fifty years. This rapid improvement in the analytical framework is all to the good, but it has created a curious situation for economic research. The crying need today is for statistical and econometric research, to put into the analytical framework precise quantitative content, which is essential for the formulation of appropriate economic policies for particular countries at particular times. Empirical research of this kind cannot be done on a "lone-wolf" basis; it requires team work, a large amount of clerical assistance of varying degrees of skill, and expensive calculating machines. In a word, it requires organized research units, and it takes money.

Because it needs organization and money, nearly all empirical research in economics is done by government departments and the handful of privately endowed research institutions, almost all of which are in the United States or the United Kingdom. Concentrating economic research in government departments has disadvantages. Such research tends to be limited to subjects that are recognized by the Cabinet to be closely related to current policy decisions. The scope and the scientific merit of the research therefore depends on the degree of economic insight of the Ministers concerned. Long-run problems and research not obviously related to current policy questions tend to be neglected. In any case, Government departments have developed a passion for keeping the results of their research "confidential". Consequently, economists outside of government are often unable to get the empirical data they need to conduct independent research, unless they have their own fact-finding organization. I speak from bitter experience. I have been a government economist, and I have been an academic economist trying to get information from governments. I have found it necessary to keep a working relationship with government, in order to be able to do useful economic research in certain fields.

Most important, lack of access to the facts makes it extremely difficult for economists outside of government to evaluate government policy, and to criticize it publicly when it seems wrong. In the past, criticism from independent economists has been a significant factor in maintaining balance in economic policy. Government monopoly of factual economic research means that independent economists, the opposition party, and the general public, are severely handicapped in their effort to scrutinize, assess and criticize economic policy. It could almost be said that an "iron curtain" is developing within the democracies with regard to economic policy.

The most effective way to combat government monopolization of fundamental economic research is to set up independent organizations capable of doing empirical research themselves. Particularly valuable today is the form of research organization set up by the National Planning Association in the United States of America. It gets funds from "Big Business", "Big Labour", and "Big Agriculture". It has agricultural committees, business committees and labour committees, each of which can publish policy statements of its own, although they seek always to reach agreement on a common policy statement. In addition, independent scholars can publish pamphlets or books under their own names, representing their own views. This form of organization has a great deal of flexibility, and it provides a means for the Big Three to meet together and discuss economic problems in an objective way, under the guidance of professional economists.

As Professor Gambs puts it:[24]

What is important today is that in the waging of war and the building of peace, the resulting economic and political systems shall tolerate freedom of inquiry. If idle curiosity can operate in an atmosphere of freedom for a few more decades, everything dear to man's utopian bias may yet be won.

Another thing the economist needs to perform his functions in a mixed economy is professional status, backed by law in the same manner as the professional status of the medical doctor, the lawyer, and the chartered accountant is backed by law. Bad economics causes more real suffering than bad medicine, bad legal practice, or bad accounting. The charlatan and quack are more dangerous in economics than in any of the other three fields. The time has come when no one should be allowed to call himself an economist, or to give professional economic advice, who has not met standards laid down by the profession — just as no one can practise medicine, law, or chartered accounting without meeting established professional standards. As in medicine, law, and

---

24 J. S. Gambs, *op. cit.*, p. 94.

accounting, these standards can be defined only in terms of a degree acceptable to members of the profession, and granted by an institution accredited by the profession. There are dangers and difficulties in this procedure, of course. Who is to decide what institutions shall be accredited, who shall determine what degree confers professional status, and who is to set the examinations for this degree? If control is left to the profession, the public remains exposed to the danger of malpractice by the controlling officials. I see no remedy for that. The same situation exists today in the other professions, and there is no escape from it. The profession as a body must decide who are the qualified practitioners, protect the public from the charlatan and quack, and help the layman to distinguish the competent from the incompetent and the scrupulous from the unscrupulous. To permit the profession to perform this service, the term "economist" must be legally defined.

This claim brings us to the fundamental question raised by Professor Knight:[25] How much *power* should experts have to enforce their recommendations? A decision as to the appropriate amount of power to accord to economists can perhaps be facilitated by pointing to further analogies between economics and medicine. Like medicine, economics is both science and art. Much medical and economic research is done in pursuit of the truth for its own sake; but the ultimate importance of research in both fields lies in its extreme importance for human welfare. Unfortunately, in both economics and medicine the science lags behind the requirements of the art; neither physical nor economic welfare can be kept at a satisfactory level, given the present state of knowledge. The gaps in *knowledge,* however, cannot be traced to lack of a *scientific approach.* In both fields, "value judgments" and mere matters of opinion are excluded from *analysis;* diagnosis, prognosis, and prescription are based upon as complete and objective analysis as is possible.

Unfortunately, severe limitations upon the methods of research are imposed by the simple fact that the subject

---

25 F. H. Knight, "Ethics and Economic Reform", *Economica*, August 1939, p. 306.

matter is comprised of human beings, who dislike being pushed around for scientific purposes.[26] Controlled experiment can seldom be used, and generalizations must often be made from a small number of identical cases. In order to conduct large-scale experiments, public sanction is necessary. "Preventive medicine" is hard to sell to the public, who tend to apply old-fashioned remedies themselves for ailments that seem "minor", to consult the expert only when thoroughly uncomfortable or frightened, even then to reject unpalatable prescriptions, but nevertheless to blame the "doctor" if things go seriously wrong. Moreover, neither Doctor of Medicine nor Doctor of Economics can wait for complete knowledge before making some attempt to alleviate human suffering; each must give the best advice he can on the basis of existing knowledge. It is right that it should be so; imperfect as his knowledge is, the doctor — whether of medicine or of economics — can give far better advice than the layman.

Considering the nature and extent of the economist's knowledge, the sort of problems that concern him, and his need for social sanction to deal with these problems, the position of the economist with regard to economic welfare is strikingly similar to the position of the medical doctor — especially the public health officer — with respect to physical welfare.[27] People want to be healthy, but there are limits to the amount of power they are willing to accord to medical authorities to *force* them to be healthy. Ultimate power in matters of public health regulation is retained in the hands of the legislature. The institutional framework within which medical doctors operate is determined by representative

---

26 "The human patient is often an inconvenient subject for experiment. He is human, and cannot be treated with severity, so the limits of any process of treatment cannot easily be found by trial. His illness makes his general physiology abnormal, so the experimenter often finds the interpretation of the effects of treatment difficult. The doctor has a natural impulse to be more interested in curing the patient than in advancing scientific knowledge. The patient has usually engaged the doctor on that understanding" (J. G. Crowther, *The Progress of Science*, London 1934, p. 291).
27 In his Sir Richard Stawell Oration for 1949, Sir John Latham, Chief Justice of the High Court of Australia, seeks to draw a contrast between the position of the medical doctor and the position of the social scientist: "The difference between the problems of science and those of politics may

governments. But the public health officer is given *legal* backing for his prescriptions in times of emergency, and is given enough legal power to deal with the more obvious sources of epidemics, communicable diseases, and the like.

Few people now regard the powers of the health officer as an intolerable encroachment on personal liberty. Much could be gained by according to the economist powers of the same order. In general, this approach means letting the electorate decide the ends of economic policy, while experts prescribe the means. As long as no other stated objective is involved, the right of the electorate to choose between higher taxes in the upper brackets or appreciation of the currency as a means of checking inflation is no more vital to democracy than their right to decide whether penicillin or sulpha shall be prescribed for septic sore throat.

It may well be true — as Professor Knight insists — that over the centuries medical doctors, in their ignorance, have killed more patients than they have cured. But who would now deny that the opportunities afforded for medical research, and the knowledge gained by according to doctors certain limited powers to enforce their prescriptions — even power to make mistakes — has been a boon to mankind? Economists, given similar opportunities, might also make

---

be illustrated by taking as an example the applied sciences of medicine and surgery. The doctor begins by diagnosis. He ascertains as well as he can the condition of the patient in relation to health and disease. . . . He then proceeds to prognosis . . . and finally he makes up his mind as to the treatment, as to the remedy to be applied. . . . All these procedures are directed to and assume the acceptance of a single objective, namely, the promotion of the health of the patient. . . . There is no doubt as to the desirability of this objective; the object is definite and clear.

"How different is the spectacle in the political arena! . . . There is no general agreement as to the nature of the welfare of society, and, as I have pointed out, even unhappiness, misery, and suffering are sometimes regarded as objects to be promoted in the course of political endeavour." (*The Medical Journal of Australia*, 8 January, 1949.)

In so far as this argument is applied to economic policy, I disagree. The description of how the medical doctor proceeds fits the economist equally well. Nor is the objective of economic policy less definite or clear than the objective of medical practice. The object of the medical patient is to stay well if he is healthy, and to get better if he isn't; the object of the economic patient is the same. And in medicine as in economics, it is sometimes necessary to inflict short-run suffering on the patient to achieve his long-run welfare, or to make some parts of the community temporarily sick in order to protect the health of the community of a whole.

wrong diagnoses, prognoses, and prescriptions. It is unlikely that they would be wrong as often as medical doctors have been in the past; economists may not be more cautious scientists than physicists, but they are certainly more careful scientists than physicians, who frequently break all the rules of scientific method by generalizing from two or three cases that fall under their observation. Moreover, the mistakes of economists are less likely to be fatal than those of physicians. If a patient dies from an overdose, there is little that can be done about it, but economic policy can be reversed. If a government raises taxes and cuts government expenditure to check inflation, according to the economist's recommendation, it does not mean that governments cannot cut taxes and raise expenditures if a recession develops instead.

If economists made no more blunders than doctors, it would certainly be desirable to give them equal opportunities to prescribe. Economic health would be improved by the preponderance of right prescriptions, and economic knowledge would grow through mistakes. Why not give the economist a chance, and let him take the same risk that a medical doctor does — the risk of losing his practice if his errors are too obvious and too frequent?